ALSO BY GARY PAUL NABHAN

The Desert Smells Like Rain

Gathering the Desert (with Paul Mirocha)

Enduring Seeds

Songbirds, Truffles, and Wolves

Counting Sheep

The Geography of Childhood (with Stephen Trimble)

ALSO BY MARK KLETT

Revealing Territory

Traces of Eden

Second View: The Rephotographic Survey Project
(with Ellen Manchester and Jo Ann Verburg)

One City / Two Visions

Ocotillo in moonlight, along the Camino del Diablo

Campfire saguaro, Kofa Range

Five hours of winter sky and petroglyphs, near Caborca

First light: ocotillo at dawn, Cabeza Prieta

Paloverde swept by breezes, Caborca

Re-storying the Sonoran Borderlands

Henry Holt and Company
New York

DESERT LEGENDS

STORIES BY GARY PAUL NABHAN

PHOTOGRAPHS BY MARK KLETT

Henry Holt and Company, Inc.
Publishers since 1866
115 West 18th Street
New York, New York 10011

Henry Holt® is a registered trademark of
Henry Holt and Company, Inc.

Library of Congress Cataloging-in-Publication Data
Nabhan, Gary Paul.
Desert legends: re-storying the Sonoran borderlands/ stories by
Gary Paul Nabhan; photographs by Mark Klett.—1st ed.
p.   cm.
1. Natural history—Sonoran Desert.   2. Sonoran Desert.
3. Human ecology—Sonoran Desert.   I. Klett, Mark.   II. Title.
QH104.5.S58N34   1994   94-18123
508.791'7—dc20   CIP

ISBN 0-8050-3100-6

Henry Holt books are available for special promotions
and premiums. For details contact: Director, Special Markets.

First Edition—1994

Designed by Lucy Albanese and Betty Lew

Printed in the United States of America
All first editions are printed on acid-free paper.∞

10 9 8 7 6 5 4 3 2 1

We tell stories to cross the borders that separate us from one another.

—Alison Deming

These stories are dedicated to Agnese Lindley Haury, for her contributions to borderlands plant conservation, archaeology, and international, cross-cultural understanding.

CONTENTS

Saguaro with shirt, at the U.S.-Mexico border

Wire rising from sand, along the Colorado River

Climber, Route 93 near Wikieup

Preface: Desert Follies and Borderline Fools

Climb up on a volcanic ridge above the dry land, look out over that vast expanse of blasted rock, blistered cactus, and stinking shrubs, their shapes wavering in the noontime heat. A word may eventually float up out of your mouth, crossing your dry tongue and parched lips. It will sound something like *desertum,* or *desierto, dizzered,* or maybe *daze-hurt.* Such a word will suddenly rise, like an unexpected whirlwind, sweeping other images away.

Desertus. A place "left wasted, barren, forsaken or abandoned," or "an uninhabited and uncultivated tract of country."

By the time you've reached the top of that ridge and scanned the horizon in all directions, such a word might gain definition. At first glance, it all looks like one huge godforsaken experiment in emptiness. "Desert," you mutter under your breath. In this case, *Sonoran* Desert, straddling the U.S.–Mexico border, a hundred thousand square miles of sparse subtropical scrub laced with giant cactus, yuccas, and other such oddities. "You came here to see that big bunch of nothing?" I heard a waitress in a small-town café scoff at some tourists one time.

We all know what she means, but at the same time, living in any desert is a kind

All at once she laughed aloud. She startled herself with the force of the laughter and wondered at its origin. For all the desolation of this place, there was a lot of life here, she thought. Nothing fancy. Basic life like the cactus and the wildflowers. Twisted life like the desert plants that had learned to live on nothing but a drop of rain a year.
—Alfredo Vea, Jr., *La Maravilla*

Todos los quelites y mezquites se están burlando de nosotros.

—Beto Nolosvea, *Captain Marvel, Desert Crusader*

of "now you see it, now you don't" proposition. While that waitress is in the "now you don't" mode, I'm sitting out here—below the ridge you have climbed—up to my elbows with the "now you see 'ems."

Somewhere down there where the dust settles, nestled behind a big mesquite tree, I'm trying to deal with a big bunch of rowdy neighbors: raucous white-necked ravens making fun of me, big-eared antelope jackrabbits who don't miss a snitch of gossip, bean-eating bruchid beetles who spoil all my food, skinny-assed coyotes who steal me blind, as well as tree lizards and pincushion cacti and other lives too numerous to mention. Humans among them.

There are some desert dwellers who are willing to admit that this place is full of other lives, but who ignore the fact that an ancient human presence is also deeply etched into the skin of American *deserta*. One such desert rat was Edward Abbey, who often climbed ridges like the one that served as your overlook. Once on top, he'd take a hit of tequila, then scrawl in his notebook a lovely, ethereal passage such as: "Light. Space. Light and space without time, I think, for this is a country with only the slightest traces of human history."

If this place was abandoned or unoccupied by humans any time since Sonoran Desert plants arrived here more than 8,500 years ago, it was never for very long. I'm constantly coming across stuff that reminds me that other people have been here for an interminably long time: a Clovis point, or "yarrahead," as cowboys here are fond of calling them; crescent-shaped stone knives for trimming off the spiny leaves of mescal; shards of painted pottery traded in from hundreds of miles away; rock-pile shrines left below arches of volcanic rock.

I sometimes see or hear other signs of life—or of death—whose origins I can't be sure about. A barn owl flies out of the tree next to me just as a Mexican Yaqui friend tells me that his uncle has died. Lights move through the desert like the headbeams on old Model Ts, then fade away, no auto behind them. I hear my name called from the edge of a water hole recently filled by the summer rains; when I arrive, only spadefoot toads are present. They're grunting, trying to mate before the pond goes dry.

There may be some pretty good reasons why you and I and the ghosts of Ed Abbey, Mary Austin, and Joseph Wood Krutch fail to hear or see everything we ought to from up on that ridge. We've probably all read in some western history book how this land has been defined by its natural poverty, its aridity, so we don't expect much. Page after page has told us about waterless, treeless stretches of the desert, of its lousy capacity for supporting other lives, those of our kind in particular. At best, such books will grant that its presumed emptiness offers a stark, sterile beauty, one that's form-fit for postcards, calendars, and posters. No wonder we carry in our heads a range of pictures that sweep out of sight any evidence that there are living, breathing homebodies down there in the Big Empty. Life has been airbrushed out of the picture, like so many scars and scratches on a bathing beauty's leg of leisure. If Nature has to be pretty as a pinup, most of us get left out of the scene.

Trouble is, most desert dwellers are too ornery to stay out of the picture for long. We're like the rake that you left out in the yard, then accidentally walked over in the dark: we pop up and smack you between the eyes.

So much for the tranquillity that many outsiders associate with desert lands. I've hung around too many *rancherías* where burros honk and roosters crow all night, and too many *tinajas* where livestock competes with wild fauna to believe I'm in the land of the serene. Light and space without time, without the traces of human history? The dark tracks of cultural histories are brilliantly illuminated in the desert; some of them glow radioactively. I've camped too many times in bombing ranges during the contrived wars of the military and heard too many cows moaning on overgrazed ranges that look as bad as the bombed ones.

The old-timers will tell you that this is the noisiest, most populous land they can imagine. It is swarming with sonorous voices. It is peopled not only by humans and their pets and livestock, but by forty-foot cacti, boojums, and ocotillo. You see the constant wave of their arms, enticing you to come over and look at what they are up to.

Giants of the cactus and ocotillo clans are not the only plants here that project their own personalities, their own strategies for rooting and fruiting in this place. Each plant here seems to have come upon its own weird ways of dealing with the heat, the drought, the catastrophic freezes, the salty or silty or limy or lava soils. When you stack it up against other deserts, the Sonoran has a wider range of plant shapes and sizes than any other desert. Roughly a fourth of the 2,500 plants here never get beyond the natural boundaries of the Sonoran region. This is their paradise.

If I have so far neglected to give animals their due, that's because the winged, legged, and tailed ones come and go, hiding or sleeping for long portions of the day. When they are active, though, they want you to know about it: the western diamondback's sudden rattle on the side of the trail; the mulling and bubbling of Gambel's quail as they drop from their overnight roosts.

It is often assumed that desert dwellers are typically rural folk who don't have the wherewithal to leave, who barely eke out a living through what they can scavenge, steal, or beg. Nevertheless, there are more warm bodies in desert cities than elsewhere in this land. On the U.S. side of the line, the Sonoran Desert is more citified than either New England or the upper Midwest. There are other residents who are not so sure they want to be out on the land. The slickers and Okies and *chilangos* and *californicadores* who have stormed into the Sonoran Desert since World War II are part of the largest human migration in history. They are a wave in the colonization and *Coca-Cola-nization* of western North America by those with European, Asian, and African blood. The *colonistas* give the place the façade of the frontier, but underneath it all are the bedrock-solid ancient cultures, *las indigenas,* who know the desert's dry spells and downpours, its floods and infestations.

Some are known as the Gila Pima, Papago, Lowland Pima, Sand Papago—they call themselves O'odham—and now farm on both sides of the border. Others are Yoe-mem—Yaqui and Mayo. And beyond are the Quechan, Cucupa, and Maricopa, with their fields along the Colorado and Gila Rivers, and the Chemehuevi, Walapai, Yava-pai, and Havasupai who live up the watersheds from them.

Not all the old cultures took to farming. Some desert dwellers remained nomadic until fifty or sixty years ago, preferring the taste and texture of wild foods or periodi-cally raiding neighboring farms during harvest time. Among them are the Dinéh—certain Apache bands who showed up just a few centuries ago—and the Kunkaak, the hardy hunter-gatherers of the Sea of Cortés coast, known to most outsiders as the Seri.

Here and there remain a few Opata, a few Paipai, a few transplanted Kickapoo. And there are other people who don't call themselves Indian, who nevertheless live as though they are natives in this land. They speak of the dirt, the rocks, the waterflows, the medicines, and the creatures with vernacular vocabularies that you can't find in any dictionary. Each of those vocabularies is probably worthy of a lifetime of study, for they tell things about the land that book-learned Spanish and English can't even approach.

While getting to know the desert intimately, these rural dwellers have left their share of *disastres, lagrimas,* and half-baked schemes all over the land. Rather than singing in perfect pitch with other desert voices, they still sound like a *norteño* band warming up for an all-night dance. They just keep on tuning up their instruments and improvising, as if no one is listening or watching. But when they stop for a moment, they may catch the reverberations of their own echoing voices or look up and see their own reflections, like mirages in the desert sky.

There is a window—or rather, a mirror—in the middle of this desert. It is called the U.S.-Mexico border. For more than two hundred miles and nearly one hundred fifty years, it has sliced through the desert's heart to remind us that the cultures on either side of the line affect this land in distinctive ways. It seldom makes us look pretty, and often makes us look absurd. We have become the fools in the desert's funhouse mirror. The stories that follow play on those marvelous distortions, the peculiar ways we come to see some subtle truths about ourselves. The image that the border mirror reveals can seldom be gained in any other light, in any other land.

I offer you, then, these desert legends, for they will help guide you in making a mental map for yourself of this chimerical land. I can only warn you that you'll be facing some thorny images, ones that may poke at you, puncture your armor, or fester within like so many cactus spines. And that you may find yourself brushing up against some wild new partners—dancing skin to skin with saguaros and ocotillos, shaking the heat of a scorching, sticky day. One of these days, when you least expect it, that festering thorn buried in your side will rise from your flesh to let you know that somehow, this place has become part of your inner workings. It may have been beneath your notice, but all the while it has been quietly leaving its mark.

OVERLEAF: Second tank at Tinajs Altas, where many died trying to find water

ABOVE: Horizon defined by light, car camping below Tule Tank

Saguaro overcome with vine, Cabeza Prieta

Ramón, Mexican farmer, Guadalupe

Ramón's granddaughter, with every can of formula and milk consumed since her birth

Boy watching spinning top, Guadalupe

Rescuing What's on the Other Side

As I write this for you, my cousins, *all of you,* I wonder if I might ever set the record straight. Snippets of your stories have already come back to me in their various versions, so I know what I am up against. On account of the ones I've heard already, I'm afraid I'm facing a stacked deck:

How the only time my mother drove out to see me in the desert, she went limp upon arrival amid all that cactus and mesquite. She later told one cousin that she simply fainted from the relentless glare of the sun. But Aunt Rose heard that she had driven one hundred sixty miles without seeing another car, only to be told at my doorstep that we were all camping out that night—it was too hot to sleep within the adobe walls. She later swore to me that she saw a rattlesnake lurking just a few feet away from where the baby crawled around on the ground. Although she didn't crumple until she had swept the boy up into the bed of my truck, she herself never touched ground here again.

Then there is the rumor that I nearly killed Aunt Linda on her only visit here, that I drove her three hours through a raging *chubasco* while water poured in through the

The central importance of entering into worlds other than our own . . . lies in the fact that the experience leads us to understand that our own world is also a cultural construct. By experiencing other worlds, then, we see our own for what it is and are thereby enabled also to see fleetingly what the real world, the one between our own cultural construct and those other worlds, must in fact be like.

—Walter Goldschmidt

¿La voz del desierto? No hay solo un voz, pues, hay un conjunto norteño. Y muchos ecos.

—Pancho Norteado

cracked glass where a roadrunner had collided with the windshield a few weeks before. When my old pickup crossed the arroyo at flash-flood stage, she claimed that water came in up to her knees—an impossibility, since there were ample opportunities for it to drain back down through the rusted-out floor of the cab. . . .

There are other legends that my brothers tell: How, innumerable times when he was alive, my father had to wire money to perfect strangers in order to get me out of Mexican jails. And how, the night my father died, they could not reach me; the lightning raging that night knocked out all the telephone and telegraph lines running from El Norte clear into Sonora.

Since no one else is with us tonight, I'll admit to you that each of those stories contains tiny grains of truth. Trouble is, they've been tumbled smooth of any texture. It's not that they're outright lies. They simply reflect how our clan worries about one of its kin. One who has strayed from the fold.

"What went wrong with him?" they wonder. "When he was growing up among us, he seemed to just love being here, cuddling up with fifteen aunts and cousins on a couch, grinning from ear to ear. But if he still does love us, then, why has he drifted so far from home? What in the world has he found that could be worth staying away from *us?* My God, he's been down in that desert nearly twenty years!"

You see, I have a problem with those stories that you, my cousins, tell. They lack any notion of what has driven me to the edge of what is familiar to you. That seemingly desolate frontier, or, as my neighbors call it, *la frontera,* is among the loves of my life. Have you ever wondered how I could have ended up loving *land* as much as we have all loved our family?

Once my heart planted itself in the dry, salty earth called Sonoran Desert, it sprouted roots that I don't think could have anchored themselves in any congested city. So even though I grew up in a clan as gregarious as ours, I now spend days on end talking only to spindly cactus and spiny shrubs. To you, they look like death on a stick—nothing like any living vegetable you know—but to me, this land is anything but barren because of them.

And that is why I have to set the record straight. I am not alone, on the bleak edge of the world. I have not been talking to myself nor merely listening to an arid wind. There are voices here among these gray, armored, ancient plants. There are seldom-seen animals which have become my guides to water, and to shelter and to other necessities I can hardly name. I now consider them, like you, to be my family. And so I spend a lot of time just listening to them, even when it seems to be no more than gibberish. It is just as I did when I was a kid, whenever we stayed with Aunt Fanny, who would refuse to speak English with me, preferring the language of the Old Country. I would listen not so much to particular words that were beyond my understanding but to the tone and timbre of her voice and to the dry and dusty places that it echoed.

THROUGH TRIALS AND ERRORS

Of course, I couldn't listen that well when I first got here. There were too many distractions, too much noise drifting in from everywhere else. And I was like the others when I first arrived. Green. A lush. Loose in my spending. Inattentive to the spottiness of pale but fertile soil, to the slightest changes in season, or to the local parlance by which they are announced. A rank beginner.

Oh, it has taken me two decades to develop some scars, wrinkles, and reserves in the right spots, to learn not to squander energy or water out of season, out of place.

At first, all I could see was that the armor looked meaner, the grass less green, the women more sensuous, the culture more contagious, and the wilderness wilder on the other side.

We use that turn of phrase a lot down here: *el otro lado*. Two decades ago, the quest for what lies on that other side became my consuming passion. A half century ago, Graham Greene articulated what is so seductive about the lands and life across the border. It was when, I believe, he was crossing the international boundary into the Mexican deserts for the first time:

> The border means more than a customs house, a passport officer, a man
> with a gun. Over there, everything is going to be different; life is never
> going to be quite the same again after your passport has been stamped and
> you find yourself speechless among the money-changers. The man seeking
> scenery imagines strange woods and unheard-of mountains; the romantic
> believes that the women of the border will be more beautiful and compla-
> cent than those at home; the unhappy man imagines at least a different hell;
> the suicidal traveller expects the death he never finds. The atmosphere of the
> border—it is like starting over again; there is something about it like a good
> confession: poised for a few happy moments between sin and sin.

Recently, while I was once again ruminating over Greene, I realized that my own view had shifted. What I once sought solely on the Mexican side of the border I have somehow come to find on the U.S. side as well. Or, more to the point, I have stopped seeking what only one side can offer me, and find this desert sticking together all around me, no matter what side I am on. Although my home has been just six miles away from an international divide that attempts to cut this desert in half, I am no citizen of the borderlands. Nope. I think I know what Douglas Kent Hall meant when he claimed that the borderland "has a national characteristic of its own, as though it were a narrow fledgling nation two thousand miles in length." Still, I can only pledge allegiance to a certain bunch of creatures, and peculiar cohort of cultures, that have somehow stayed in sync with the underlying desert of Greater Sonora—that is, parts of Arizona, a sliver of Alta California, the bulk of Baja, and the state of Sonora itself. I'm not saying this desert never feels caged up with political boundaries; I only reckon it will outlive them.

Let me say it in another way: that fence cannot divide those of us who live on either side. We need one another. That's why we gather on flyways, migration routes, and underground railroads. We've learned to outmaneuver governments. Oh, they can hinder us, but I doubt they'll ever halt our flow.

And when it comes to how we feel about this fence, I am not just speaking for myself and a few radicals. I also speak for the *paisano,* or what some here call the *tadai,* the *churea,* the *correcamino*—that rakish roadrunner who hops up on a strand of barb-wire stretched between two republics, wags his tail, shits, and darts over to the other side. I speak for the nectar-feeding bats—the ones that in summer hang out in old mine shafts across the border during the day and squirt red all over my toolshed at night. I speak for *las familias* Antonio, Elias, Tanori, Vasquez, Corrella, Ronstadt, Escalante, Alvarez, Cruz, Meling, Murrieta, and Valenzuela. The ones of O'odham, Dutch, Cucupa, Hispanic, Dinéh, German, Opata, Lebanese, and Yaqui descent. They have their cousins on both sides of the divide.

Finally, I speak for a wild gourd, with a vine that crazily twines over the razor blades marking the top strand between here and there. I've watched that vine, how it seems to pay those blades no mind. It crawls across them, then dives to the ground, rooting itself from the nodes wherever it touches the earth.

A MISPLACED VISION

I don't have visions often. I have never sought them, never will, and I remain highly suspicious of anyone who does. But let me tell you about one such apparition I had a few years ago. I was driving out to work in some Indian bean fields, grinding along the road that runs parallel to the border between Tucson and the Tohono O'od-ham Reservation to the west. That's where it happened.

All I can say is that it lumped into one single image all that I had been imagining about "the other side" until that time.

I woke up early that morning when the stars were still brilliant. The remaining cool of the night made me shiver as I entered my truck and began to drive out to Papaguería—that's the old name for the country of the Tohono O'odham, both their reservation and the surrounding turf they got swindled out of. A cup of hot *café combate* steamed up from my lap, enough to fog up the windshield. I finally had to crack open a window to let the temperature inside square off with that outside, so I could see where I was going. All the while, night moved through twilight and then on to dawn.

When the sun began to brighten the day, I had made it out as far as La Avra Plains. Its low-angled beams suddenly warmed the air out on the plains, but the heavier pockets of cool air were still tucked down, out of reach in the arroyo beds below. As I swallowed the last dregs in my cup, and glanced toward the Altar Valley southwest of me, sun spilled into that heavy air mass. A number of buttes and mesas loomed up before me. There, on the desert grassland rim between the Atascosas and Baboquivaris, mirror images of Sonoran landforms tilted up upon one another. They created hourglasses out of pyramidal buttes, and anvils out of flat-topped mesas. I just dallied there on the road-side, dumbfounded, as they wavered in front of my eyes, as if a wind were shaking them. There they were, quaking in the heavy air, which was as instable as quicksand. Then they toppled and, just like that, fell back below the horizon forty or fifty miles away in Mexico. Gone. Gone from view in a split second.

It dawned on me: I had been seeing most everything on the other side in a wildly distorted way. Each giant cactus, each hacienda, each mountaintop shrine on the Mexican side of the desert had become exaggerated. Each culturally charged image had become a mirage by the simple act of looking across a political boundary.

BRAIDING RURAL LIVES BACK TOGETHER

As this specter vanished from my sight, I moved the truck back onto the asphalt and hightailed it to the reservation. I sweated through that day with old men who wanted to fix up their fields, which had been left in disarray. These Indian farmers knew what they were doing, or wanted to do, but it was still no easy feat. We figured out that the dirt in their fields had been turning poor, starved of what Sonorans call *agua puerca,* "hog water," so called because it carries suspended vegetable and animal manure. Some cattlemen down by the border had built water impoundments upstream, forgetting that the old guys down here needed the floods to run into their fields. Without floods to bring the hog water, with its enriching detritus, into their fields, their beans and melons and maize had begun to wither and wane.

We tried to make up for this loss the hard way, hauling truckload after truckload of manure and mesquite litter into their fields. We'd go to a nearby corral, or a "cattle lounge" beneath a big mesquite tree, and shovel the dark rich stuff into the truck. Then, when we tried to find a tractor or a team to plow under the manure, our luck ran out. The John Deeres out there had seen better days, and there was not a spare-parts store for another hundred miles. And no one with draft horses had the proper tack for hitching a team in front of a moldboard plow.

"Where did you get tack for your teams before?" I asked one of those old Indian men, taking my sombrero off and wiping the sweat on my brow.

He ruminated for a moment, then answered me: "We used to have our own *hihilio*. What do you call them, *herreros* or blacksmiths? Some of them were tack makers and horse doctors too. Some were so good at fixing up horses that we let them fix us up too when we got cut up or sore. A few became *O'odham mamakai*, our medicine men. Now they're all gone, so whenever we break our plowshares or lose our tack, we have to go over there"—he nodded southward—"to Jujkam Ha-Jewed [Mexican's earth]. If we don't cross to the other side to get what we need, we can't farm."

Their farming tradition had unraveled when the intrusion of the border cut their homeland in two. First there was the Gadsden Purchase in 1853, which gave some of them U.S. citizenship, but which began to wean them from practices thoroughly Mexican. Then, in the 1930s, the governments decided to put up a fence along their imaginary line. The fence had enough gates in it and got washed out frequently enough that at first it didn't stop the trading of cattle, horses, squashes, *queso asadero,* and other goods.

The hoof-and-mouth disease quarantine finally nailed the lid on the coffin. Fearing that the intermixing of livestock from both sides of the border would further endanger the American cattle industry, U.S. officials forbade the Arizona O'odham from riding down to the ocean on their salt pilgrimage, to Magdalena on the pilgrimage for their Saint Francis, or to Stoa Doag to gather cactus fruit for summer ceremonies. Then they rounded up five hundred horses and cows, shooting, burning, and burying them near the village of Komelik. Several hundred more were massacred on the other side at Pozo Verde.

"That was all we had to our names—like your savings. Except we *knew* those animals. The smell was so bad, it spoiled the air for miles around. One old man cried, 'Why don't they go ahead and shoot us too?' "

In villages where eight teams of horses and mules had worked together to keep the fields plowed and cultivated, suddenly there were none. The farming families who couldn't stand to see their fields fallow drifted off to work in the irrigated cotton fields that southern whites had begun around Eloy and Picacho. Back home as the 1950s drought hit, the dry ditches filled up with debris, the check dams atrophied, and tumbleweeds overran formerly productive fields.

On the Mexican side, there remained enough horses, blacksmiths, mule skinners, and tack makers, but not enough O'odham who had the seeds and knew the prayers to sow the fields, to keep the rains coming and the ditches clean. Young men in Sonora heard that they could get real cash for doing the same work that, up to that time, had only offered a winter's supply of food. They, too, wanted what was on the other side, as badly as I had wanted to live the adventures, dance with the *guapas,* and sing the words to old *corrido* ballads when I discovered Sonora in my twenties. They left home to find work in Arizona lettuce fields the same time I left home for Sonora, to find the ancient seeds, the hand-forged plowshares, draft horses, and stories.

While most greenhorns felt this way about the other side, the older men felt that to be whole again, their pueblos needed to repair the fabric ultimately essential to both sides, to stitch it together once more. It was not simply their tack or their seeds that had fallen into disuse. The broken, unraveled cords of their lives needed to be braided together again. Somehow, I got it into my head that I could help with that braiding. My cousins—*mis primos*—that's why I'm still here.

Night storm over Glendale

Night-blooming cereus hiding in creosote bush nurse plant

Cactus placed on International Boundary marker

Border fence cut by flash flood

Looking south toward Mexico on the Camino del Diablo

Boy with toy gun, border town, Mexico

Cryptic Cacti on the Borderline

HIDE-AND-SEEK

While driving along the U.S.-Mexico border one scorching hot August day, I found myself falling under the spell of mirages once more. For starters, I had been letting my dreams drift toward a few scattered clouds. I was secretly shaping them into thunderheads, hoping that they would bring rains. I craved thunderstorms and the relief they carried with them; the air-conditioning wasn't working in my Jeep, and salty sweat was stinging my eyes, blurring my vision. On top of that, I had a headache pounding like a misfiring piston, making me more miserable than on most desert rides.

I was crabby, too, because it had just sunk into my weary brain that the ancient cactus stand that I had been wanting to survey wasn't in good shape. A few decades ago, someone went and put the border fence smack dab through the middle of it. Later, the Feds bulldozed a road next to the fence on one side, and the Mexicans bulldozed another on the other. I sensed that it was suffering other insults as well, insults I would soon learn about firsthand.

Up to that time, I had figured that the border fence was a pain in the tail only for

Un arbol en el desierto es menos asombroso que el hombre por los arrabales, bajo la lluvia, cubriendose con un periodico.

—Jose Lezama Lima, *Las Eras Imaginarias*

A tree left standing in the desert is all the more astonishing considering that every man in the suburbs wishes to cover his head in a newspaper, every day, come rain or come shine.

—Juan Hoidkam, *Urban Dysfunctional Literature and Its Meaning to Trees* humans and other migratory animals who had to cross it on a regular basis. Now, I reckoned, it was even wreaking havoc on sessile creatures like cacti.

I was supposed to be hot on the tracks of a night-blooming cereus cactus, *Peniocereus striatus,* which was considered to be a rarity. It is never that simple: when I followed the historic surveyor's notes I had been given, and walked the distance from the fence as specified, I ended up in the middle of a rutted road. I forgot about the directions and began to wander through the scrubby hills and valleys beyond the roads.

If any cacti were somewhere around there, I had not been fortunate enough to find many. Within the past ten months, I had found a measly seven plants south of the boundary. Slim pickings after more than fifty hours of cruising on foot through their suspected desert haunts. As I wove up one slope and down another, hitting upon one cactus every seven hours or so, I thought of the blues lyric, "If it wasn't for bad luck, I wouldn't have no luck at all."

The Sonoran cereus are cryptic, hiding their lead gray stems deep within the thorny mess of gray branches of the few desert trees and shrubs that offer any shade. You hardly ever find them out in the open. As if being in the shadows, nearly invisible, is the best way to survive this stinkin' hot desert. It must be, because they've given up the best defense that other cacti have stuck with—they lack needlelike spines to keep intruders away.

Instead, these spineless cactus stems are the same color, shape, and diameter as those of the creosote bushes all around them and not too different from the branchlets of ironwood and wolfberry. This coincidence has spurred cactomaniacs to talk of "cryptic coloration" and "protective mimicry," as if each cactus decided that it would be more fitting to cross-dress and live its life in drag.

It doesn't make much sense to me. Cryptic coloration must be aimed at fooling rodents, jackrabbits, and bigger browsers like desert pronghorn—discouraging them from eating a vulnerable cactus if it looks like an oily, unpalatable shrub—but most mammals are color-blind. I'm color-blind, too, but the seven cacti I had seen far outnumbered the ones that many of my color-sensitive buddies have scared up in the same amount of search time. All I know is that Sonoran cereus are harder than hell to see even when you've walked by them a dozen times.

After years of searching by various hapless biologists, only sixty plants had been found in the lands along the two hundred miles of Arizona-Sonora border falling within the Sonoran Desert. Multiply that batting average by my crabbiness quotient, and you can understand why my mind was turning every cloud into a harbinger of rain: I longed for relief from this heat and reprieve from my fruitless searches.

That August day, I was to have my two wishes granted: for rain, and for more Sonoran cereus cactus. By the time my Jeep had bounced down the rutted borderline road to reach the hills where I had seen the first seven specimens, a stray storm cloud had lingered long enough to dump a half inch of rain in a matter of minutes. Though it failed to turn the road into a running arroyo, the downpour was good enough to dampen the dust and drop the temperature below a hundred degrees for the first time in hours.

My headache lifted. Maybe it was the sudden rush of ozone in the storm-charged air. As my crabbiness began to disperse, I decided to circumambulate one rocky knoll once more, not far from the few plants I had already discovered. The entire scene had been transformed by that scant half inch of rainfall. The brief deluge had darkened the lead-colored stems of the creosote bush to a charcoal black. Beneath them, the Sonoran cereus cacti were showing their true colors as well. A powdery bloom had been washed away from the cactus stems, revealing a brighter green. Dressed up as dead sticks moments before, the cereus had suddenly broken dormancy. Water had reached their roots for the first time in months and triggered their internal workings. The plants were breaking bud, but better yet, a miniature forest of cacti was instantly revealed between the rain-washed trees.

As quickly as the green cereus stems could reveal themselves against the black background of the surrounding shrubs and trees, I added plant after plant to my cactus count. In forty-five minutes, I spotted eleven additional Sonoran cereus, some of them under creosote, but others beneath small ironwood and paloverde trees. With the help of the rains, I had all of a sudden become a hundred times sharper at cactus hunting than I had been in all the previous months of the dry season. I had finally tracked down enough of the cereus on the Sonoran side of the line to compare their situation with that of their Arizona brethren a few hundred yards away.

DIFFERENT SIDES OF THE FENCE

The rains continued that summer, bringing the good as well as the bad with them. The bad was my once-white Jeep getting mucked up regularly in the puddles along the borderline road. The good? I was able to tally up more than one hundred and ten Sonoran cereus plants on both sides of the border. Still not much cactus, considering that I had looked under every bush within a two-mile stretch along the border, going back at least another half mile on either side of the fence.

One day, while leaning up against the fence to tie my shoe, I began to ponder whether this cactus was naturally rare or merely a victim of what was known as the "borderline effect." I paused a moment and stared at the fence between my two study sites—three strands of barbwire that marked the boundary between two sovereign nations with capitols in crowded cities thousands of miles away from this desert. Those metal strands of barbwire shimmered in the desert heat. I suppose they were meant to be symbolic of political division; they didn't serve as any real physical barrier. I could hop across them in a flash. I'd seen roadrunners zip through the wire and jackrabbits duck under it plenty of times. A buddy of mine once saw a Sonoran pronghorn jump clear over the highest strand without missing a step.

But the crazy thing was that the fence had started to shape out a clear "ecological edge." Soon after those strands of barbwire were pulled taut by some cowboy's come-along, the ways people treated the desert diverged on either side.

I plucked one strand of barbwire, as if twanging out a chord on a huge steel guitar. This ecological edge was not identical to the line of the fence but reverberated around it, like the afterimage of a guitar string struck, then watched until its sounding ceased. I was beginning to sense the fluidity of the borderlands—how phenomena on one side of the fence affected those on the other—rather than simply seeing one side cut off from the other by a static partition.

The ancient plants on both sides began their lives as one thinly scattered stand; now they were fragmented by the presence of the fence and the roads that run on either side of it. Trouble was, I had been ignoring how that demarcation had changed the uses of the land following the Gadsden Purchase in 1853. Perhaps two-thirds of the locally known cereus plants had become U.S. citizens, while the others remained under the flag of Mexico.

Before then and for some time after, I suspect that the plants and the people around them were not much affected by international politics. Historically, the O'odham Indians were just as sparsely scattered in the area as the cactus. For centuries, desert life moseyed along for them, more constrained by heat and drought than by the land-use trends in either country. Even the Hispanic families who colonized the region continued to run cattle in both countries. Gradually, however, the U.S. and Mexican economies went their separate ways—former partners on opposite sides of the fence were forced to split the sheets. And each left his own peculiar imprints on the desert.

One of those imprints was in the shape of a hoof, and it sank deeper into Mexican soil than it did on the American side. Overgrazing was the norm on both sides for decades, until the U.S. government agencies began to force the Indians and their neighbors to reduce the size of their livestock herds. To this day, overgrazing in northern Mexico seldom gets held in check by anything more than the severity of droughts, which periodically decimate the wild *corriente* cattle hiding out in the brush-choked canyons and arroyos.

I had seen the effects of browsing and trampling by herds of cows, goats, or horses just the other side of the border, but I began to pay more attention to overgrazing of the desert scrub where the cereus grew. It was clear that livestock had browsed back much of the shrubbery beneath which the young cacti took cover. At the northern edge of its range, cereus cactus seedlings need more cover than farther south in frost-free areas.

Had the Mexican cattle snuffed out the hideaways required by the cereus? Sonoran cowboys run stock in densities two to five times higher than the desert's carrying capacity—that estimate I could confirm simply by walking around, year after year, watching how much vegetation was being eaten away. But what is odd is that borderline overgrazing can be seen even more clearly from thousands of miles away.

Waiting to have a beer with a buddy in Tucson one summer, I prowled around outside his office, looking at pictures on his wall. There it was, in a photograph taken from a satellite with infrared film: my little cactus survey site! The Mexican side of the border had been so badly denuded that I could see the border as clear as day. My friend later explained it to me: less red south of the line meant reduced plant growth on the Mexican side. He told me that climatologists up near Phoenix had figured out how the border had even changed local weather patterns. Where trampling and browsing had left the soil more barren and dry, wind speeds have increased markedly while ground temperatures have risen several degrees on the Sonoran side of the fence. These harsher conditions make it tougher for seedlings to get established. If they do survive, the maturing plants remain vulnerable to a variety of stresses.

I suppose I could have stopped there and blamed all the world's ills on cows. But I soon began to grasp that grazing was not the overriding pressure throwing the desert out of kilter. I had noticed that legume trees on the Sonoran side had scars from wood-cutting on their trunks and branches. I decided to tally up the damaged trees, and in one week, I counted forty-eight trees with cut-up trunks or branches on a seven-acre hillside. The next week, when I arrived to tag those trees, I found that nine more iron-wood trees had been cut in the previous six days. Down in the washes below the hill, the cutting had been even more aggressive—stumps stood bleeding in the open where massive canopies had once offered shade. Woodcutting was dramatically decreasing the plant cover in which cacti could hide.

I was just beginning to fathom that deforestation in deserts can be as devastating as overgrazing, but it took me more months of reckoning to realize that the two threats were not unrelated to each other. For some reason, I thought that the local woodcut-ting was for nearby grills and hearths of low-income Mexican households. As displaced *campesinos* from Mexico's south gravitate to the borderlands in the hope that American prosperity will rub off on them—or take them in—they build shantytowns in the desert lands harboring slow-growing trees. Border towns in the Sonoran Desert have grown sevenfold in size since 1950. In their borderland barrios, nearly all the fuel used is taken from wood collected within walking distance of the *campesino*'s tar paper, cardboard, and plywood shacks. The desert's low yield of kindling is used for everything from heating tortillas to keeping flimsy-walled homes above freezing during winter nights. The stumps I saw, bleeding out their last gasps of sap, were victims of fallout from the borderland's population bomb.

Around this time, my Mexican friend Humberto Suzán helped me figure out what was going on. He immediately doubted that all the wood being cut was going for local home use. As tallies of pruned trees and stumps filled our field notebooks, we realized that well over half of the legume trees within reach of the cactus stands just south of the border had been cut back or killed by woodcutters. It wasn't long before we observed trucks coming down the borderline road with wood stacked ten feet high. The boys riding along with each load told us that the wood was destined for expensive restaurants in border towns adjacent to national parks, where American tourists came in for mesquite-grilled steaks and seafood. They themselves had only recently taken up woodcutting after the fields they had been working in had succumbed to whiteflies and to the prohibitive costs of pumping deep groundwater for irrigation.

What surprised us most was that the surge in wood gathering for restaurants had used up most of the local supplies formerly available to the shantytown dwellers, who could not match the firewood prices that the restaurant owners paid. Suddenly, the poor families along the border were forced to search for kindling in the United States, where professional woodcutters could not drive their trucks. The locals waited until it was close to dark, then illegally ducked under the fence with borrowed ax or rusty saw and cut an armload of wood in the U.S. reservations, refuges, and parks across the border. In one federally protected area, there was just as much woodcutting going on in its washes within two hundred yards north of the border as there was on the Mexican side of the fence. About a third of the legume trees still living had ax marks and saw scars, and three-fourths of the stumps we encountered were cut remnants of ancient trees that had not been given the chance to die natural deaths.

The borderline *campesinos* were hauling back home a variety of desert legumes for firewood, but I was surprised to learn from them that paloverde had become one of their mainstays. Compared with ironwood and mesquite, paloverde seldom receives praise as a fuel, and yet it was suddenly commanding prices of eighty-five dollars a truckload in the nearest Mexican town.

I asked one old Mexican cowboy about this. He grumbled, indignant, "I'd never buy paloverde if I had a choice. Paloverde is so punky, it burns as poorly as toilet paper." He reiterated that the mesquite he favored was being used up as charcoal and as fuelwood in barbecues and grills, but that another high-quality wood had also vanished—ironwood.

As these ancient trees have been cut up or burned, night-bloomers and a dozen other kinds of cacti—from towering saguaros and cardons to miniature pincushions—have been left without the protection of thorns and shade they depend upon. For a Sonoran cereus, having a woodcutter blow your cover means certain death.

INTO THE THICK OF IT

Not too much later, while talking with several border town woodcutters, I learned that new markets had opened that were taking all the ironwood they could carry. "What markets?" I asked. "Well," one of them replied, staring at the toes of his cowboy boots, "all the remaining ironwood within an hour's drive of the border is being used to make 'Seri Indian' wood carvings. You know, carved animals to sell to American tourists."

"Why are the Seri Indians needing ironwood from up here on the border?" I asked. "Their villages are four or five hours to the south."

The group let my question hang in the air and went back to work. Later one of them took me aside and explained the situation to me. None of them had seen any "real" Seri Indians in years, but their wood was still going to make "Seri carvings." Then he smiled mischievously and added, "There are at least a thousand other Sonorans making carvings like theirs to sell to the tourists! An awful lot of instant Indians, no?"

The woodcutter was admitting a fact that few American tourists had fathomed: the majority of "Seri carvings" they were buying were not made by the Seri at all, although they were often advertised as such. Since the mid-1970s, the market for Indian carvings of animals had boomed, and nearly every Mexican beach town from Mazatlán clear up to the border now had non-Indian craftsmen who chainsawed, then carved and sanded ironwood by machine. The Seri themselves, who had begun selling handmade carvings to tourists a decade before, had lost out to this competition—only a tenth of the one hundred fifty carvers among the eight hundred remaining Seri still made ironwood figurines with any frequency.

The Seri had found that they could not undercut the prices that the machine-assisted carvers could offer to tourists, for it often took them a week of hand labor to make a carving their competitors could crank out in an hour. And the Seri preferred to gather only the dried ironwood on the desert floor, from long-dead trees. Woodcutters were now selling their competitors six giant ironwood trunks for one hundred fifty U.S. dollars, cut from live trees that were four hundred to twelve hundred years old. As wood became scarce near the carvers' villages, the cutters raised their prices even higher and ventured inland to cut virgin stands of ironwood. When non-Indian wood-cutters began to be caught on Seri lands, clandestinely cutting live ironwood trees, the Seri arrested them and complained to government officials that they had had enough.

On a summer day Jim Hills and I drove the Sonoran coast into Punta Chueca, a Seri village that he had visited hundreds of times over the previous quarter century. He was not "Jim" to the Kunkaak people who lived there. He was "Santiago," a man who had clowned around with them, learned to sing their sacred songs, flirted with the community's women, and traded tools for carvings with two generations of Seri. They embraced him, tugged at his arms, pulled at his Hawaiian shirt, and teased him about how long it had been since his last visit, how poor his memory for Kunkaak vocabulary had become, and how many women were pining away for him.

Then, when someone mentioned competition for ironwood and crafts markets, the crowd calmed down and listened intently. "Why would anyone buy the Mexican carvings?" asked Ernesto Molino, a craftsman whose production had declined in the face of all the imitations. "We can shape animals so that they have a life that the Mexican carvers could never copy."

We sat around and threw out some ideas of how to deal with the dilemma. Finally, Santiago stood up and invited the Kunkaak of Punta Chueca down to the town of Kino Bay to meet more formally the next day. "If you don't like talk, at least come down for some food. There'll be a feast for everyone who comes." We got in his truck and left a trail of dust behind us.

The next day, the patio outside the Kino field station was loaded with Seri families, some shaping clay into figurines, others looking at carvings made out of barite, a stone that they carved when ironwood could not be found. Gradually, attention shifted to a table where Pedro Romero, the tribal governor, had invited his neighbors to voice their concerns over the depletion of trees central to their traditions and the resulting loss of economic options.

By the end of the afternoon, more than eighty of the Kunkaak had signed a petition to the Mexican government that explained how they had lost their livelihood, selling carvings of desert and marine animals that were part of their traditional lore. The mass production of machine-made ironwood carvings and the clandestine and excessive cutting of ironwood and mesquite for charcoal production were singled out as the major causes of that loss. The one government representative present conceded that it was time to legally protect the rights of Seri artisans and agreed to begin the paperwork to do so.

I looked around the table at men and women who had lived most of their lives beyond the reach of electricity, television, books, and power tools. They knew the movements and postures of dozens of animals so well that they could effortlessly shape them from wood, clay, or stone. I read down through the names on the petition, some of them signed by recently schooled children for elders who had never learned to read or write: Rey Morales Colosio, Rosa Montaño, Carolina Morales Astorga, Enrique Romero Blanco, Roberto Molina Herrera, and so on. Here were people who knew the animals—bighorn and quail and Gila monsters—ones just as likely as the cacti to be extirpated should the ancient desert forests disappear. No trees. No animals. No stories. No carvings of the animals in the stories. *Domino.* That simple.

WHAT FLOWS ACROSS THE BORDER?

Back on the border, I stumbled upon a hacked-up ironwood, with a heavily browsed night-bloomer beneath it, its young stems hacked back near ground level. The next month, it was gone. Such premature deaths have become a sorry fact of life in Mexico. I reckon they occur far more frequently there than *al norte,* on the other side of the fence.

That fact should leave no room for smugness among American environmentalists, as if night-bloomers north of the border are a whole lot safer. Not by a long shot: the fates of the cacti in both countries are as intertwined as the strands of barbwire strung out along the dividing line.

When I first went looking for those spindly cacti, it was during the winter, when they were dormant. Devoid of flowers, fruit, or any frills. It took me a while to really believe that night-bloomers are hot items up North, where such exotic flowers are painted, planted, and panted over by the horticultural bourgeoisie.

Let me put it bluntly: they had the cuddle appeal of dead sticks. And so I snorted at the notion that anyone would want them for their greenhouse or front stoop. Even if they wanted to bag one and take it home, I doubted that they would go to as much bother to find a few plants as I had.

Then, in late August—not too long after the rain and its revelation—I stumbled into a cereus population just after dusk. At first, from a distance, I thought someone had left some flashlights on, dropped out among the desert scrub. As I walked closer to some ironwoods and creosote, the flashlights beneath them turned into flowers. I couldn't believe my tired eyes.

"*¡Sonababíchi!*" I exclaimed to myself. I had lucked upon one of the four or five nights that they would bloom that entire summer.

They were gorgeous! The ugly ducklings had metamorphosed into swans! Silky white trumpets drenched with a perfume that I could smell before I could see some of them. The way the delicate buds and flowers were splayed out on the stems reminded me of some fancy floral arrangement in a Japanese painting.

In fact, the jazziness of night-bloomers had not been lost on Japanese floral fanciers. Black-market cereus cactus have been smuggled into Japan and sold for upward of ten thousand yen. No matter that the cactus trafficking is in violation of CITES—the Convention on International Trade in Endangered Species—wealthy hobbyists hold that agreement in contempt anyway, as if they're the only ones who know what is good for rare plants. Night-bloomers not only are flown into Japan but arrive in Germany and other northern European countries as well. The wilder they look, the more they cost.

Where were these plants coming from? I had a hunch that some were being dug up at a few of the places that scientists were naive enough to mention in popular journals. Some cactophiles have even published detailed maps to rare plant localities. More often, one hobbyist hand-draws a sketchy version to give to another cactus collector, who in turn passes it on to other friends. The inroads made by pioneering scientists had become rutted with the heavy tracks of corrupt collectors.

To make matters worse, most cacti are dug up on the lands managed by the government agencies that have the strongest conservation messages—the National Parks and Monuments, National Forests and Wildlife Refuges. I suppose they get visited more than the lands handled by the Bureau of Land Management or the state, but they must get more than their share of "git-me-one" tourists as well. Tourists to Sonoran beach towns also bring a mess of cacti back across the border hidden beneath seats, in the hulls of boats, or inside tires. Throw a bunch of empty beer cans and smelly trash on top, and the border guards let them sail through rather than wallowing in the smell.

From the plant's perspective, who owns the land or what country it inhabits doesn't matter. But over the long haul, night-bloomers growing near the limits of one landholding remain dependent on those living beyond such limits. The Sonoran cereus is seldom found in densities greater than five plants per acre, and they are often spread thinner—a single plant over several acres. Their prime habitat may cover only one hundred twenty acres per square mile.

They don't know who owns them when they start to grow—and the land can change hands several times over a century. Their habitat may be accidentally split between two countries or two land managers, and no one tells them.

Where I staked out my survey with Humberto, we stumbled upon seventy night-bloomer plants on the Mexican side of the border and another forty-five on the U.S. side. Other than the hundred-fifty-acre home ground where all these cacti cluster, there is no good habitat for a considerable distance in either direction.

Small patches. Low numbers. Low densities. Watchers of Sonoran cereus worry. Why? Because these guys need to be cross-pollinated to make any seed. Let me put it another way: if some pollinator does not find two plants blooming the same night within reach of each other, the whole effort is fruitless.

I wonder how they do it. About a third of all the plants in the stand bloom simultaneously on any single night, then close shop the next morning for good. Over the whole season, a single plant may have blooms on three or four nights, but hardly more than half of all the plants set any fruit at all. And many that start to ripen bite the dust before they turn ripe.

Now, put yourself in that plant's position: if you were a cereus flower, you would have less than eight hours of your whole blooming existence to attract a moth who has already visited one of the fifteen to twenty other bloomers scattered all over God's creation. If the moth fails to show, or carries no good pollen your way, you fail to pass on your genes. If you are a U.S. cereus, and a third of your mates are wiped out on the other side of the border, your chances of making sprouts become mighty slim.

Your meager supply of mates within reach may be enough of a worry, but what if your moths are being knocked out as well? When your cactus population sits smack dab in a valley with twenty-five thousand acres of irrigated cropland in it, some bugs around you will go with the flow. But what do you do when the five hundred acres closest to you are put under the plow and into cotton, and three thousand gallons of pesticides are sprayed out of a plane right when you come into flower? Sex under such conditions begins to look like risky business.

Remember the good old days? No lack of mates, no paucity of pollinators? Well, now your most frequent visitor is a common desert dweller, the white-lined sphinx moth. That's the good news. The bad news is that its larval form mobs irrigated fields as a notorious summer feeder on cotton foliage. The cotton farmer thinks that your sexual go-between is his biggest pest. The Parathion, Thiodan, and Azodin he's squirting on his cotton fields are aimed at controlling sphinx moth larvae—your connection for a hot date.

My mind is weary of trying to think like a flower. One notion after another has initially escaped my comprehension, and now this one—having a pollinator that is naturally abundant but attracted to cotton fields is a kiss of death. Why? The moth larvae become thick enough to attract pesticide sprayers.

The night I finally caught sight of a few sphinx moths buzzing from one cereus flower to the next, diving in from yards away, I had reason to relax. At least I could be sure that during that one summer, on that particular night, there were enough pollinators splashing about in this small binational gene pool to keeping it flowing, from becoming too turbid. The sphinx moths had not yet been drenched with insecticides. There was still hope, perhaps, that the untamed desert nearby was still expansive enough to harbor enough moths to the service of this small cadre of night-bloomers.

Jazzed up, I took my friends, my wife, and our children out to see the last bloom of the season along the border. We were in luck, on time to be dazzled by the floral flashlights shining up from under the skirts of desert bushes. As the moths zipped around us, we spotted several additional night-bloomers that we had walked past numerous times but could not see until they were in bloom. Once again, patches of gray, static shrubs were transformed, for we could see the blossoms, freshly opened and fragrant, attracting an orgy of bugs, beetles, and moths.

By nine in the evening, it looked as though most of the pollen ceremonially offered up that night had already been spent. Exhausted ourselves, we began the bumpy ride along the border down the puddled, muddy Mexican road, overwhelmed by the chimeric nature of the desert: one moment seemingly barren and lifeless, the next, its garishness unmasked. Had I been sleeping, or had the desert?

A haze hung in a cool air pocket as the Sonoran road crossed a muddy arroyo. As my Jeep lumbered up out of the depression, I thought I saw through the mist a cluster of men in the middle of the road. With instruments? In the heavy air and in the beam of the headlights, the men looked as though they held trumpets, violins, *bassos sextos,* and *guitarrones.*

"Mariachis!" I cried, startling the half-asleep passengers in the Jeep. As we peered through the windshield into the haze, the trumpets turned into pistols, the *guitarrones* into Uzi machine guns. An antidrug patrol, well armed, was on the prowl for loads of marijuana and cocaine.

"What are you Americans doing down here in the middle of the night?" the head of the Federales asked. He seemed bewildered by the presence of children in the vehicle.

"We've been out smelling cactus flowers," I tried. The chief grimaced, unconvinced.

Where cultures collide on the border, even cactus sniffing carries its own risks. As the odor of dust and firearms filled the Jeep, the fragrance of the cereus flowers vanished from our midst. We were like the cereus, caught without cover. If only we could reach across the border, reach and suddenly find some refuge. But the hope of immediate refuge drifted away like smoke, and we were frightfully exposed.

Passing a tequila truck along the border road, Mexico

Artifact from a rough road, Mohawk Valley

ABOVE: Bedspring patio fence, near Sonoyta

OVERLEAF: Bras decorating a juniper, Christmas Tree Pass

Hanging Out the Dirty Laundry

A RUDE AWAKENING

Most everything I've learned about the desert has come from rooting around in the wrong place at the right time. With that method, I've caught whiffs of news about desert life that I'd never get by reading all those travel brochures, tourists guides, and fancy maps dolled up for those who fly first-class. When I want to go deep into the desert, I don't take a plane; I begin on the ground and head down from there. And because ground travel means that I've got to get visas, car insurance and permits, pesos, and other such paraphernalia if I am to travel in Sonora, I inevitably do time at the local border crossing, going through those rites of passage that citizens of one country have conjured up for those of another.

Despite years of practicing those rituals, I always seem surprised to have ended up on the other side of the line hours later than I had originally expected. By that time, the light has begun to fade, and the chances of reaching my ultimate destination at a decent hour have grown slim. I often decide to drive until I am just too tired to go any farther, and then I look for a place to camp that is tucked back a ways from the road.

Trouble is, by the time I decide to call it quits, most cues to comfortable camping

Once upon a time, taking out the garbage was an event in our lives. . . . We were part of the rituals connecting us to the earth, from the places food grew, through our houses and bodies, and then back to the earth. Garbage was real, part of creation, not an objective invasion of cans and cartons. . . . We are the garbage, the waste, we make it and dump it.

—Gerald Vizenor, *Landfill Meditation*

Hace trienta años que he vivido en los dompes, entre el desperdicio y la recolecta . . . por encima de la basura, los perros muertos y los metales escondidos, pero bajo el olor, bajo el humo, bajo las almas tratando de escapar. La basura es mi vida, mi trabajo, y el unico recurso que tengo para sobrevivir.

—El Pepenador, *Guia a Los Dompes Sonorenses*

sites are already gone. Even if there are pulloffs, *rincones,* or side canyons in which to hide, the best ones are already taken by truckers, gypsies, or thieves.

For such reasons, I have been forced to sleep in places I would not necessarily choose were my eyes wide open, my pockets not empty, and my head screwed on straight. And as all of us proclaim after we have survived a rotten time or place, I have become a richer man for it.

I remember one particular morning after my sidekick and I had first been detained at the border, and then at an all-night fiesta we had stumbled into—one that had engulfed the entire town of Magdalena, Sonora. When we finally escaped the traffic and the crowds, we desperately wanted to sleep away from the beams and horns and grinding gears of semi trucks. To make things simple, I drove a mere two hundred yards beyond the last lights on the edge of town and headed my truck off a rutted dirt road into a dry wash. There, a few trees would shield us from the lights and noise of passing revelers. Without even looking around, each of us immediately threw out a sleeping bag and tarp, unfurled them, kicked off our boots, crawled into the flannel-lined warmth of our bags, and closed our eyes. We would postpone the worry over how to get out of the sand until the next morning, when we might have our wits back together again.

My wits remained scattered through the night and into the following day. The cocks at the nearest ranch began crowing around four in the morning; a braying burro wandered through camp and nudged me awake. When I finally dared to open my eyes to meet the passing of the *madrugada,* the twilight, I was instantly unsure that I was ready for the day.

All around me, in the muted light of the hour just before the dawn, I could make out patches of color hanging from the bushes and the lower branches of the trees.

Being botanically inclined, I first thought "Flowers!" but no, something was wrong; late fall was the wrong time of year for a peak in blooming. So I glanced around once more, trying to get a better sense of the textures and shapes as well as the colors. I noticed glitter, dazzle, ruffle, lace. "Christmas tree decorations?" I wondered. Yet I could not for the life of me figure out why the local folk would bedeck hackberry bushes and cholla cactus with such gaudy ornaments, for the holidays were still a month or so away.

Then, as I pried my eyelids fully open, the flamboyant forms came into focus: fire-engine red panties, pink fishnet stockings, leopard-spotted bras, baby blue boxer shorts, and tinsel-glittered pantyhose. I rolled over and looked up the wash a ways: still-turgid plastic bouquets, Fruit of the Loom jockey shorts, red-flannel long johns, and cologne bottles were strewn hither and yon, tossed down from a low hill that overlooked the arroyo where we camped. I took a harder look at the adobe buildings up on the hill, and they appeared a bit peculiar for a Sonoran ranchstead—it was something about the red lights running around the windows and doors.

We were camped in the *dompe* of the local house of ill repute, on the edge of the *zona roja,* what many of you may think of as civilization's hinterlands. The inventory of brilliant forms exposed in the wash suddenly made more sense to me. In fact, that was the first time I had ever come to read trash, trash which served as a sign for the wild life that had come before me in that place. And now, it is clear to me that such trash has made my life a whole lot richer.

READING TRASH

Learning to read trash may be easier in the desert than anywhere else in the world. For one thing, junk hardly ever gets hidden in the desert, because the few bushes and trees tend to keep a healthy distance from one another, leaving a lot of room to see the trashy texts in between. If you go down south to the tropical jungles, or east to the Atlantic seaboard, you witness such a muddle of rank growth that your sense of the land is obscured. The whole place is so choked with trees and other vegetation that trash is soon out of sight and out of mind.

A friend of mine, a farmer, recently drove that point home to me. Pedro had worked the vegetable fields of New Jersey when he was younger, but about a decade ago, he came out to the deserts of Arizona and southern California to grow flowers for the nursery trade. He soon learned that there was one big difference with the way he had to deal with crop residue in his new homeland.

"Back in New Jersey, I would make a pile of the toughest *paja*—cornstalks and cobs, squash vines or bean pods, stuff that doesn't take to compost too well—and I'd leave it back in the woods wherever I could find me a little opening. By the next summer, it would be grown over, and by the next fall, it would have made itself even scarcer. But down here, if I left the same threshings and winnowings out in the desert, they would be visible for years!"

The trouble with rubbish in the desert is that it barely decays. The rain is so slight, the dirt so poor, that a good, quick rot cannot be taken for granted. Oh, the sun can bleach the daylights out of colored cotton, melt a plastic bottle, or buckle and tan a piece of hide, but most organic garbage in the desert is dreadfully slow to decompose.

In 1861, an engineer named Raphael Pumpelly was given a strong lesson about the lack of decomposition in the desert. He stumbled upon the strangest of sights on a brilliant moonlit night while riding the Camino del Diablo. The Camino had been a major route of the California gold rush. He was approaching the Tinajas Altas—a chain of tiny rock-lined tanks between Quitobaquito Springs and Yuma, Arizona—

when he and his horse became spooked by what lay ahead of them: "Suddenly we saw strange forms indefinable in the distance. As we came nearer, our horses became uneasy, and we saw before us . . . a long avenue between rows of mummified cattle, horses and sheep."

He tried to make sense of this parade of the dead. "The route over these wastes is marked by countless skeletons . . . and the traveler passes thousands of carcasses of these animals wholly preserved in the intensely dry air. Many of the dead, perhaps for years, had been placed upright on their feet by previous travelers. As we wound . . . through groups of these mummies, they seemed like sentinels guarding the valley of death."

Pumpelly must have been struck dumb by this ghastly apparition, but his fellow traveler, Charles Poston—a man later named governor of the Arizona Territory—simply tried to explain it away, knowing all that he did about the Camino and its desperadoes. Still, the image would not leave Pumpelly's mind; he wrote about it twice. "Nothing could be more weird," he admitted. "The pack animals bolted, and Poston and I rode through with difficulty. Ten or twelve years before, during the time when meat was worth in California almost its weight in gold dust, it paid to take the risk of losing on this desert nearly all of the herd if a few survived. If no water was found at the tinajas, most or all of the animals and some of the men would die. In the intensely dry and pure air, there was no decomposition. All the dead simply became mummies. The weird avenue had been made by some travelers with a sense of humor and fertile imagination not [already] deadened by thirst."

Though I have never run into such a traffic jam of beef jerky out in the desert, I have noticed other desiccated remains and have duly recorded them within the hundreds of pages of field notes I have written at garbage dumps, butchering sites, and trash pits. In the debris left behind by any family or tribe, I can see a sort of script that they acted out, a signature as legible as a carcass left open and marked by wolves.

One of my favorite places to go and read trash is Quitobaquito Springs, right on the U.S.-Mexico border, a major pit stop on the Camino. Since 1978, I've found everything there from *ballenas* and *caguamas* of beer and freshly filled Pampers to ancient piles of Sea of Cortés shells, chert arrowheads, cremated bighorn bones, and obsidian flakes. I've also spotted broken *metate* grinding stones, cast-off rinds of Papago pomegranates, and riggings for a shallow well. These latter leavings reminded me that the land downstream from the springs was farmed for centuries because it could draw upon one of the few constant trickles of water around.

Once, when I went with friends from Quitobaquito toward the Sea of Cortés coast, we happened on a place where O'odham pilgrims must have gathered shells for making jewelry and sacred salt for their ceremonies. Hoping to reach the ocean, we had been hiking for hours against a stiff wind when we decided to take a breather in the shelter of low dunes next to the barren mudflats that lined our path. I guess we had been surrounded by mudflat mirages and other illusions so long that abandoned shrimp boats and dead trees appeared to float above the watery horizon. We were thirsty for a substantial sight, and after a half day of scanning the flats, I had tallied up only one heron skeleton, three owl pellets, a couple of fish tails, and a scatter of coyote tracks. Finally, we hit upon a prehistoric shell midden, one that stretched for a full half mile along the slopes of a low dune. There, the O'odham had discarded millions of clam shells. Compared to remains of bighorn, cottontails, or doves, those spent bivalves were found in an abundance unparalleled anywhere in O'odham territory.

Other than the shells of clams and scallops collected for ornament, I found only a handful of potsherds dispersed across that dune ridge, plus an occasional clump of salt crystal that had been transported up the slope as well. Not another trace of humanity riddled those dunes.

From the mudflats and dunes, I jogged with the wind at my back to railroad tracks a few miles inland, a place where freight trains stopped to rewater. It was a desolate outpost called Lopez Collada, named for a railroad worker lost in a sandstorm decades earlier. There, in the midst of a blinding sea of sand, the rubbish on the surface suggested that not a single morsel of food had ever been locally produced—it looked as though everything eaten there had been brought in from miles away. The sand was littered with *salchicha* weiner cans, tequila bottles, egg and coconut shells.

I walked along the railroad tracks, searching for whatever remains of other manly pursuits—there were no signs of women's trash—that the drifting sands had not yet fully buried. I struck upon a few monstrosities: oversized iron rack-and-pinion gears from Caterpillars or cranes. I also reeled in a few rarities: huge crystals of sea salt and shriveled-up fish skins from someone's forays to the coast. Every deposit spoke of the dirty work of a male-dominated world: motor oil vats, driveshafts, *Hustler* foldouts, and rubber boots. Still, what summed up the essence of the place was a field of abandoned but uncorroded mattress springs: signs of a land so lonely that basic creature comforts had been shed, so dry that even rust dies of thirst.

POLLUTION AND PREJUDICE

Unfortunately, I've found that my penchant for rural Sonoran trash piles disgusts many of my fellow travelers and colleagues, especially those accustomed to the neatness of parks and suburbs. Listen to this tirade from curmudgeon Ed Abbey: "Sonora. Northwest Mexico. Land of the open-air beer joint and the shade-tree mechanic.

More old cars upside down than right side up. . . . Around every house, every building, lies a glittering field of broken glass, painful to the eyes. Though the barefoot kids, the snot-nosed *muscositos,* dash across it without a moment's hesitation. Can an entire nation, even a poor one, take on the appearance of a garbage dump? Yes, easy, every yard, street, and roadside is littered with broken glass, rusted tin cans, shards of plastic and shreds of rope, rubber, paper. Laundry hangs out everywhere."

A thick slice of Mexican trash does get loose, but even when it reaches bins, the average Mexican family dumps about a third more trash than the average American family. It took me a while, however, to figure out why that statistic told only half the story. Before American food gets vacuum-sealed into envelopes and freezer bags, it is stripped of all its peels or trimmed of all its skin and fat at some distant packaging plant. While American garbage cans contain more packaging, their contents compact easily. Mexican cans harbor all the debris that goes with growing or buying fresh food: bones, bean pods, corn silk, husks and cobs, carrot tops, the outer leaves of cabbage.

Despite the reduced volume of trash in the garbage cans in front of their homes, North Americans and western Europeans consume 80 percent of the world's wealth and leave behind 75 percent of its waste and pollution. We can nevertheless pride ourselves on how neatly we do it.

We North Americans have constructed the world's most concentrated sanitary landfills—one of them is over one hundred fifty feet deep, holding three billion cubic feet of refuse—but they hide from our eyes how many resources we let slip through our hands. The toxics in our desert disposal sites seep down into the groundwater in such heavy doses that they are poisoning wells in south Tucson and central Phoenix. These chemicals have been blamed for high rates of cancer and birth defects in the barrios and ghettos that surround the landfills and toxic waste dumps. Nonetheless,

American society remains haughty about its superior capacity to contain and conceal all of the dangerous residue it produces.

Of course, Mexicans are up to their elbows in problems as well, because only sixteen of every one hundred pounds of solid waste expelled from their border towns are promptly taken to the municipal landfills which the government sanctions and supposedly controls. That means that every day, in the desert border towns alone, another 2,700 tons is burned or left on the streets, or hauled to one of the ragtag dumps on the barrios' outskirts.

On the edge of one border town—Sonoyta, Sonora—some of this refuse falls into the hands of my friends Victor and Manuel. They have lived in *basureros*—as dumps are called in urban Mexico—but now seem resolved to spend the rest of their lives in this borderland *dompe*. There, they get to glean what American tourists forget, what thriving local businesses discard, and what *mojados* departing for farmwork in the United States leave behind them.

The first time I met Victor and Manuel, they knelt to warm their hands over the flames rising from a smoldering "boom box" radio on a chilly winter day. They were melting it down to sort its worthless plastic and steel shell from the resalable copper inside it. Their genius is in knowing what to sort, and how, in order to find diamonds in the rough. All over Mexico, these guys are called *pepenadores,* a term rooted in an ancient Spanish verb that once described the way certain vegetables were picked from the ground and sorted. In Mexico today, the word is more frequently used to describe the way the homeless pick through garbage to rescue the remaining kernels of value hidden within the chaff. For Victor and Manuel, the kernels are usually made of copper, aluminum, and bronze, since these metals can be sold by the pound to men who come around from recycling centers in Mexicali and Phoenix.

"We get good days and bad days, like anybody else," Manuel sighed, standing up and stretching his back. "But here, at least I can do my work for free."

"For free?" I asked, not understanding what *libre* meant in this case.

"You know, without having to pay any *cacique* some kickback. Where I worked for a while in Mexicali, I had to pay the *pinché dueños del dompe* something for the right to rescue what they would have buried otherwise! At least here I can gather whatever I want without having to pay nobody nothin'!"

I glanced behind Manuel, as he bent back over his campfire, and noticed all the things he had gleaned for his ramshackle cabin. He used a light post, curtain rods, a bumper, and telephone poles for cornerposts and *viga* crossbars. Over this frame, he had lashed down fenders, tarps, sheets of black plastic, plywood, mattresses, rugs, and door frames to make walls and a roof. To keep them from blowing around too much, he stacked fruit crates against the walls, wove saguaro cactus ribs into a latticework, and piled tires, deer antlers, and two-by-fours across the roof. He said that he'd already gotten his hands on a far greater range of goods to build with here than he had when he lived for a while under a bridge in L.A.

Unlike Manuel, Victor had never spent much time on the other side. He had lived on the edge of Sonoyta for twenty years and had wandered across the desert enough to figure out where little patches of wild plant foods and medicines grew. He was the one who would walk a mile and a half to the river to get water in a plastic jug when they could not talk truck drivers into hauling fifty-gallon drums.

It had been raining lately. They had spread out pots and pans around the yard and on their roofs to capture water for their animals and themselves. This would spare Victor from playing mule for a trip or two down to the river.

"After Christmas, business will pick up. It's our best time of year, I guess," Manuel said, looking to Victor for agreement.

Victor nodded. "The American tourists who pass through here to go to the beaches, they leave behind lawn chairs and other things that we can fix. And," he added dryly, "there are people here in Sonoyta as rich as those in America. Those *ricos,* they buy everything new at Christmastime, throwing out perfectly good furniture and clothes just because they are a year old. Now that's what we like to see."

A sudden movement on the hill above their makeshift homes caught my eye: it was the wingbeat of a vulture who had been sunning himself on the top of a saguaro cactus. The *zopilote* lifted off from his perch and swooped down over part of the dump where one of Victor's dogs—suffering badly from the mange and from open wounds—lay still on her side. The mongrel raised her head slightly, staring at the *zopilote.* Not dead yet, she seemed to say. The *zopilote* turned around and flew back to his perch. He would postpone his own recycling project until it was clear that the mongrel could no longer raise her head.

RECYCLING JUNKIES

Sometimes when I have huffed and puffed my way up top a ridge of lava near our house, I have seen a smoke plume rising a few miles south, across the border at the spot in the valley where Victor and Manuel live. "What a frickin' shame that they burn all that stuff," a hiking partner once complained to me, as we caught our breaths and watched the plume drift toward the national park on our side of that border. "All that pollution. All those *natural resources* gone up in smoke. The visibility is getting as bad here as it is in Phoenix."

Until I began to chew the fat with Manuel and Victor, I hadn't reckoned on how little trash they actually burn compared with all that arrives in their yard. When a new load of rubbish comes into the dump, the *pepenadores* usually aren't the first to mill through it. They often keep hogs—not as pets but as coworkers—and these hogs root around in the piles until anything and everything edible is chowed down. With all the slops that get dumped in a decent-sized *dompe,* a hog can put on pounds in no time, so the *pepenadores* get themselves some pork now and then. More often than not, though, they sell off the biggest hams when they need to buy staples. I've even seen them flag down a passing truck to haul a sow into town to sell on the spur of the moment—if one of their many cuts gets infected and they need a doctor to get medicine quick, swine serves as their bank account.

Those hogs start the presorting process too. A Mexican friend of mine claims they're so smart that they nose all the junk into separate piles. The hogs are followed by older men, who get the first crack at collecting any unbroken beer and soda bottles for return to the local *deposito.* They also riffle through the piles for salvageable clothes, tools, or accidentally discarded prizes: watches, lighters, or flashlights that may still work. If they wish to rescue heavier finds, they call in the younger men, who haul off any reparable furniture, usable lumber, brick, iron, or tin.

At that point, the pile is left to dry out for a few days, before it is torched and reduced to essential rubble. That is when the bulk of the *pepenadores* return with their digging bars, mining the rubble for precious metals. Along the way, they pack down the charred debris so that it serves as an access route, ready for the next truckload and its attendant hogs.

As another truck rumbles into the yard, I've seen a dozen vultures get up from the roost next door and soar. They'll then circle together over the smoldering piles for hours on end. They remind me in no uncertain terms that scavenging should be seen as among the most ancient and decent of professions, one that has been needed as long as waste has been generated in this world. Scavengers, as I see it, are those who turn the upward curve of consumption back onto itself. They help complete the loop that allows the rest of us to go on living.

CELEBRATING WHAT IS ROTTEN

I suppose that from time to time, we have to face all the waste there is in our own lives. It's tough. Most folks would rather do anything than confront how much we squander. American society has become adept at vacuum-packing old foodstuffs into stories-deep landfills. For some reason, we'd rather do that than let those scraps nourish other animals. We have become stingy with what we are willing to pass on through the food chain, and so we leave less and less room in this world for scavengers, saprophytes, and detrivores. But without them, nothing is returned. If we burn crop remains rather than allowing them to ferment in compost heaps, we lose an opportunity to fertilize our fields and gardens. If we don't fertilize the crops on which we depend, there will soon be too little food for all those cuddly, fuzzy herbivores that we try to model ourselves after. Look at suburban society today: it has become so sanitized that it barely allows for the existence of death and decay.

Fortunately, I seldom see that phobia for decay in other cultures. Some folks have always known that their own survival depends upon returning organic matter back to the earth. Desert people celebrate cloudbursts not only for the water they bring but for the rotting and release of nutrients that they trigger as well. Desert people savor the smell of the rotting detritus that washes into their fields carried by summer flash floods. They have come to associate that fragrance of fermentation with a future abundance of food and mention it in their prayers and songs to bring fertility.

In their rain-bringing rites, one group of desert Indians, the O'odham, speak of *wako'ola,* the nutrient-rich floodwash which we now know is the key to the fertility of their desert fields. In the first translations of O'odham songs for bringing rains and fruitful harvests, Anglo-American professors assumed that this term meant any kind of trash, flotsam or jetsam. An O'odham friend of mine was appalled when she read a transition of one song. "Here I was, reading this wonderful poetry, then I came to this part about *trash* that didn't fit in with the feeling of the song."

In fact, the song referred not to *any* old trash but to windrows of legume leaves and stems, rabbit manure, and composted weeds. These gifts are carried into fields by the summer floods, where they are later plowed under to renew the richness and moisture-holding capacity of the soils. Mirroring what would happen in their fields, desert dwellers have traditionally fermented the fruit of giant cacti. They drank this wine while singing of the rains and their fragrant floodwash. Not so much wine into blood, or wafer into body, but decaying plant matter into soil, soil into plant, new fruit into wine, and wine into song. That's how they closed the cycle on their calendar year in the middle of the desert summer.

For years, I mulled over my Indian neighbors' heartwarming embrace of decomposition and decay, their fascination with fermentation, their ritual enactments of how the world must come full circle to let new life germinate and grow. I yearned for a way to express the same sentiment in my own cultural symbols, in some modest ritual of my own.

About that time, I read in a little paperback called *Seeds, Spades, Hearths, and Herds* about some "dump-heap theory" of the origins of civilization. It was written by a geographer named Carl O. Sauer who had spent time in Sonora in the 1930s. He had decided that early civilization had been fueled by the energy and fertility of the dump heaps that surrounded frequently used campsites. That was where the first plants were domesticated, for gourds and amaranths and cannabis favored such settings. It was not that someone domesticated these plants; rather they domesticated themselves by adapting to the episodes of disturbance and decay on the edges of the camps. Later, those who used these plants realized that they could sow their selected seeds into other dump heaps and trash piles, and increase the amount of food produced close to home.

Sauer's theory sounded pretty good to me, especially because it fit what I had seen around Indian camps in Sonora and other places in Mexico. Still, I failed to take it too seriously until one fall, when I went plant hunting down the west coast of Mexico.

Near Tepic, Nayarit, I finally found my way to immortalize our putrid beginnings. There, atop a *basurón*—one huge heap of rotting debris—I gathered a botanical specimen that I now consider to be my most prized contribution to the world of botany. It came from a gourd vine that grew luxuriantly from the broken-open fruit discarded during the previous year. It spread out over the ten-foot-high heap of vegetables, yard trimmings, and sweepings. Its delicate tendrils, drenched in slops, had wrapped themselves around potsherds and bottle caps, pieces of broken glass and rotting food scraps. Rather than wresting them from these embraces, I pressed the vine, the flowers, and the tendrils, with all their trashy attachments.

When I returned north and had to cross the border, I decided to declare the entire ensemble as a donation I was making to an American museum. The plant inspector at the customs station was leafing through my plant press, when he stopped to scrutinize my latest botanical find, replete with accessories. It was trapped between two pieces of soiled and stinking paper and had kept its acrid fragrance. He then glanced up, gave me a good hard look, and muttered, "That's the damnedest thing . . . you mean to tell me some museum might wanna put some putrefying trash on exhibit?"

"I sure hope so," I replied. Then I muttered, "It's about time we honored what is rotten with this world." Just then I looked out over the piles of paper, through the window of the customs office, and caught sight of a plume of smoke curling up from the local *dompe*. A flock of vultures caught the same thermal and rose in a spiral around the smoke. "Ah, *zopilotes,*" I thought to myself as I cinched up the plant press and left the border crossing behind me. *Zopilotes.* The true Phoenix birds, rising from the ashes.

Discarded target, White Tank Mountains

Woman with portrait of the Virgin, Querobabi

Abandoned doll with nurse plant, Darby Wells

ABOVE: Lizard caught by ocotillo snare
RIGHT: Feet of mortar, decaying sculpture at Driftwood Charlie's Camp

Searching for the Cure

When I'm under the weather, I get this clammy feeling inside my body. It is followed by an urge to be cured by the heat of the Sonoran sun, cured by the hands of some sun-dried elder, cured by a faith in notions beyond the immediate understanding of my one-track mind. It is then that I search to recover part of me that may have been left on the other side.

I knew this ancient, bent-over, teetering, white-haired woman who lived in a small pueblo miles past the line, whom I believed to have the wherewithal to help me. She had grown up on the Chihuahuan side of the Big Bend along the Río Bravo, where she raised a fairly big family. She moved to Sonora a decade or so ago, after her husband, a physician and faith healer, had passed on. In Sonora she settled beneath a hill she planted full of her medicinal plants—aloes, magueys, nopales. She fixed up an old adobe and reared loads of herbs in recycled *Nido* formula cans that lined her patio and hung from the rafters. There she commenced to minister to the many walk-ins who sought her out, in much the same way her husband had done east of El Paso.

I had been suffering from a burdensome fatigue and soreness in my ankles for several months, and had gotten no decent help from highly schooled medical doctors. The day I decided to look her up, I drove miles through creosote flats to where she lived on the edge of a dry riverbed. It was the dead heat of midsummer, and the rains

Esta afición por experimentar la había heredado de su abuela, una india kikapú . . . Entonces el abuelo le había construido este cuarto al fondo de la casa, donde la abuela podía pasar la mayor parte del día dedicándose a la actividad que más le interesaba: investigar las propiedades curativas de las plantas . . . En él [cuarto] John había pasado la mayor parte de su niñez y adolescencia. Cuando entró a la universidad dejó de frecuentarlo, pues las modernas teorías médicas que ahí le enseñaban, se contraponían enormemente con las de su abuela y con lo que él aprendía de ella. Conforme la medicina fue avanzando, fue llevando a John de regreso a los conocimientos [de] su abuela: ahí encontraría lo último en medicina.

—Laura Esquivel, *Como Agua Para Chocolate*

were still nowhere in sight. Storm clouds were starting to pile high over nearby mountain ranges, but there in the valley the little humidity simply kept us all rumpled and sticky. A cloud of dust followed me into her farmyard, passed me as I slammed on the brakes, and descended upon the *curandera*'s plants. I got out, dusted myself off, and walked into the fierce midday sun.

When I stepped onto her patio, sheltered by a makeshift roof and a hundred hanging herbs, the temperature dropped a dozen degrees. A pleasant mustiness hovered in the air. In the shadowy calm of her little oasis, I could take my sunglasses off for the first time all day.

"*Buenas tardes,*" I announced to no one in particular. Soon, a young man in his twenties—her grandson from town, an apprentice, I later learned—appeared at the screened doorway to her kitchen and curing room.

"*Me gustaría obtener la ayuda de la viuda. La viejita. La señora de la casa . . .*" I said, fumbling. I didn't want to use the word *curandera,* even with her family members, for in these parts it still carries with it the curse of *brujería,* wicked witchcraft.

He looked me over, up and down, wondering why in the hell some *Hombre Blanco* might show up for his grandmother's help. He had seen only Mexicans and Indians come around before, and wasn't even sure that her curing worked on White People. "*Abuela, un señor, pues, un Yori, le gustaría platicar contigo.*"

"*¿Donde está el?*" A faint voice arose from the inner rooms of the adobe farmhouse.

"*Atras, en la sombra. ¿Sería mejor platicar en el patio, o aquí en la cocina?*"

"*Pues, en el patio, mi'ijito. Un momento, por favor . . .*"

Soon, the white-haired woman teetered out onto the patio and let her eyes adjust to the shadowy light there. She spotted me, offered me a bench, and took a seat on

"Everything we need for healing is found in our natural surroundings," doña Felicia told her, and put her two hands in front of Caridad, palms facing her. With those two hands she had repaired more bones and muscles and rubbed out more intestinal obstructions than you could shake a stick at. Yes, those two wrinkly instruments of ancient medical technology were in the final analysis all doña Felicia could count on.

— Ana Castillo, *So Far from God*

another beside it. She put me through a rather formal interview, I suppose so she could decide whether or not it was possible to help me. Although a few of her terms were obscure to me, we proceeded mostly in Spanish. I learned later that she had some rudimentary English that did her little good in curing rites.

I mentioned that I had come once before, bringing an old arthritic man from an O'odham village a hundred miles away, a man who had heard she could relieve his arthritis, and who had been satisfied by what she had done. I also knew a daughter of hers who lived in a nearby town.

She smiled politely, then touched my hand. "Well then, why do you come here now?"

I explained to her my affliction, rubbing the places where the vagrant inflammation arose, underscoring the bags beneath my eyes, and admitting that Western medicine had left me less than confident that I had the malady under control.

She listened carefully, her eyes wide open, looking into mine the entire time I was speaking. I noticed something striking about hers: they had a sky blue outer ring, but toward the retina, they turned an earthy greenish-brown. They were penetrating, but not in an aloof, analytical way; they meant to me that she was searching me out to see if her skills would even work on someone from another culture.

She sat quietly for a minute, her pale, wrinkled hands clasped in her lap, her gaze reaching off into the distance. She sighed and turned to me, feeling my wrists, ankles, and chest with her hands. There was a kindness to her touch.

"I believe I can help you, as long as there are no clouds building up above the house . . ."

I assured her that the only visible clouds were over the mountain on the far eastern horizon.

"Well, that is good. I require the sun's energy to help me with my work. For some reason, this gift of healing that has been given me is weakened on cloudy days."

She's living in the right place, I thought. Eight inches of rainfall, fewer than thirty overcast days the entire year. She sighed again and stared me straight in the eyes.

"My gift, it came before I was even born. When I was still in my mother's womb, some wild animal came howling outside our house on the Río Bravo. Wolves or coyotes, I don't know. They say I heard them, and shouted from the womb three times! When my mother told this to my grandmother, who was also a *curandera,* she said it was an omen of the gift I would have."

I must have looked unsettled, for she touched my hand again.

"Some say that I must be a *bruja,* bewitched, for that to have happened to me, but I am not. I simply believe that with faith, anything is possible: we can purge the pain and evil out of lives. That's right! Smoke it out! That's what I do! I have had to help people who were hurting so badly they were carried into my kitchen. When they left my care, they were walking and smiling. Still, I cannot take full responsibility: the sun, the full moon, the saints, the herbs, the stones . . . all assist me."

"There are still no clouds . . . but is there anything else we need today?" I asked.

"Alcohol to burn! I am out of alcohol with which to make the smoke. Could you go get some . . . any kind . . . *aguardiente, mescal, sotol,* or plain cane alcohol. Yes, that might be best. La Victoria brand. Find it in a pharmacy or liquor store, and return here within the hour before the clouds come."

I returned forty minutes later with some bootleg bacanora mescal in hand, as well as a storebought bottle of La Victoria. The widow looked at both, smelled them, set the mescal aside, and chose La Victoria for the tasks of the day. She had placed a chair between the stove and the kitchen table, parallel to them; it faced a frying pan on the

floor, another on the edge of the table, a menagerie of saints on her hutch; her working area was surrounded with additional pictures of baby saints, candles, bottles of
cologne, and now, two kinds of alcohol. She poured some cane alcohol into each frying pan, paused, then began looking around for something else.

"May I help you, *señora?*"

"I can't find the little stones . . ."

"Are they alone?"

"No, I believe they are together in a little bowl, but I don't see it. You need to hold
two *piedras* in your hands while I cure you, or else . . ."

As she tottered around the kitchen, I imagined that I had come upon a *Méxicana*
version of Merlin, prone to forget the magical formula of the day, or worse, mistake it
for another. Both of us looked around the kitchen for the bowlful of pebbles for
another few minutes, with no luck. Then I heard something, and peering out the
screen door, saw her daughter drive up—the one I had met before. So I went out into
the yard and asked if she knew where the stones were. She came into the kitchen and
found a bowl full of translucent rocks above the stove. Relieved, we proceeded.

"Dos piedras por cada mano." She poured into each of my hands two pieces of rock
salt. "Hold them tightly, and then when I command you—'Burn the *sonababíchis!*'—
throw them into the flames. Afterwards, we'll see what shapes they have come out of
the burning and melting, okay?"

"Okay . . ." I was uncertain that I would understand the symbolism, but of
course, that's why I came for the help of an elder. I never have been able to figure out
much of that stuff on my own.

She had me sit down in the chair, facing the saints, the herbs, the candles. She put
out the lights in the room, except for two candles. Then she stepped behind the chair

in which I was sitting, put her hands on my shoulders, and began calling on the presences in the room, *beseeching* them, I guess:

"Most powerful, with you, with faith, nothing is impossible to cure. So please help cure this one who has come for our guidance. Please purge from him those who have made him sick, and leave him well again."

Then she began with the laying on of hands, all the time reciting creeds and *dichos* she knew by heart. She pressed her palms firmly against the top of my skull, my forehead, eye sockets, cheeks, chin, mouth, throat, shoulders, forearms, upper chest, and finally, against my heart. She stood before me, looking straight at me with her gentle, bicolored eyes, and repeated her laying on of hands. I remember the feel of her hands upon me. They surprised me with their firmness and strength as she pressed them into my shoulders, back, and chest, but they were also soft and warm when she touched upon my eyes, mouth, and heart. As she patted me, praying, I fell into a deep, relaxed state.

It was then that I had a muscle spasm in my lower back; I leapt a little in the chair. A sudden jump.

She stopped for a moment, drew back, and looked at me curiously. "Did I touch a soft spot in you?"

"There was no pain, if that's what you mean. Sometimes when I relax, after running for instance, my back jumps like that. It might be from an old injury—when I was thrown from a horse . . ."

"No," she said, laughing softly. "This was something different I think, something good. Did you see the woman shoot out the door when you jumped? She left you when I caught her out of the corner of my eye. She's been making you feel uneasy, no?"

"Some female spirit left my body?" I said, flabbergasted.

"She left this room altogether! Didn't you hear the screen door slam? Let's continue . . ."

She stood before me, holding my wrists and crossing my arms back and forth upon my chest, all the while maintaining her incantation, "*Con fé, todo es posible . . .*"

The *curandera* then instructed me to stand up and placed me before the frying pan. She had me roll up the pant legs of my dungarees, then she rolled down my sweat socks and held my ankles for a moment. "Now it will be easier to smoke out the pain," and with a flick of her wrist, she lit a wooden match and launched it through the air. It cascaded into the pan on the floor, where the alcohol burst into flames. "It's time for you to cross the barrier of fire," she spoke, and she stood on the other side, motioning me to come.

I went bowlegged, duckwalking over the flame and smoke. My temperature soared. I sweated and trembled. The heat waves rose up before me, my view of the *viuda* wavered. I reached her, and she took my shoulders, turned me around, and commanded, "Cross over to the other side, again and again. Hold the stones tightly, and let them suck up all the pain that is being smoked out of you."

I moved slowly across the flames that lapped up around and between my legs, gripping the rock salt in my hands, and suddenly, a cool breeze wafted over me. It then occurred to me why I was there.

It had been a fuzzy notion in the back of my mind until that time. But now it was burning clear. I had to rid myself of a residual sadness about past failures with others, failures that had been clouding my life. To absolve the guilt and disappointment that had plagued me, to disperse nagging preoccupations I had about what I had done to make myself sick, I crossed the flames five, seven, maybe a dozen times—trying to burn the clouds away—before the widow pulled me from my reverie.

"Shake the pain out of you! Toss it into the fire! Flick it off of you like this!" She motioned for me to rub it off of my clothes and skin, to wring my hands out and dump the residue into the pan of flames. I brushed myself as if I was taking a whisk broom and clearing dust and debris from my pants and shirt, and letting any gunk that came off me feed the fire in the pan.

"Now take the little stones in your hands—they have taken up the remaining pain—and throw them into the flames! Cry out! Burn, you *sonababíchis!* Git outa here, you *sombrábagun!* Tell them to leave and never come back!"

I don't know how loud I shouted, or for how long, but soon the stones were gone. I blinked as their melting salts sizzled in the pan, and another wave of relief came over me. I stood next to the *viuda* and watched the flames die down. She asked me to pick up the pan with a pot holder, and bring it to the stove so that she could see what residue was left.

"Oh, see how they've burnt. We've gotten them, no?"

She peered into the pan from different angles and laughed quietly to herself.

"Yes, we may have gotten them all . . ." and then she said a word I could not have understood—it sounded like *vinotellos,* the yeast-laden residue left over after wine making. I repeated it, but she shook her head. So she tried to explain. "Inside of you are little beings—like *pichilingis*—I don't know what you call them in English. But they try to take charge and play tricks on your body. They are who we are after! To purge them from you, so that you can recover!"

She then splashed some rosewater into my hands. She had me dab my eyes, neck, throat, and wrists with it, until its perfume pervaded the air.

"Lift up your shirt now, and apply this to your belly and chest!" I cupped my hands, and she shook some herbs drenched in cologne into my palms. I splashed it all over my upper body, then dried my moist hands on my calves and ankles.

"Good! Now, don't bathe or wash for a day. It will take some time for the rest of them to depart, but don't you worry, they will go. Thank you for coming. You know, I haven't had too many patients lately."

I tried to hug her.

"No, *ahorita,* no. I am a little weak. Not now. Anyway, you're still curing. *¡Vaya con Dios!*"

"Igualmente." I left her some pesos under the bowl of rock salt and handed her a necklace full of *milagros*—little copper *ex voto* effigies of hearts, legs, eyes, and ears. If family members were hurting, my Sonoran friends would often put these trinkets in the care of the saints who stood around their shrines. They decorated the statue of Saint Francis in nearby Magdalena, and adorned the shrine of El Tiradito in Tucson. The old lady was clutching the effigies against her breast as I left.

With that, I returned back across the border. Getting home, I felt so drained that I could hardly stand up—punch-drunk, I think they call it. I went to bed and slept a good twelve hours—a deep, painless sleep, no dreams, no fits, no spasms, no aches all night long.

I awoke the next morning to the sound of the whole desert dawning outside my window: Gambel's quail, cactus wrens, Gila woodpeckers, gilded flickers, curve-billed thrashers, and white-winged doves hooting up a storm. I sat up in bed and felt the sun and still-cool morning air filter through the window screen. That was the morning when the two sides of my life began to congeal. Something had begun to cure me deeply. Like hides tanned by being steeped in a dark infusion of oak or acacia bark, then pulled to dry in the full sun.

ABOVE: Adobe maker's feet, Querobabi
OVERLEAF: Marker where a family of eight died of thirst traveling the Camino del Diablo

Canal built to move water across the desert, Central Arizona Project

Mexican migrants drinking beer at the site of an inscription by Fr. Marcos de Niza

Trailer, Cargo Muchacho Mountains

Shuttling Across: Weaving a Desert Serape

"Hay una frontera que sólo nos atrevemos a cruzar de noche," había dicho el gringo viejo. "La frontera de nuestras diferencias con los demás, de nuestros combates con nosotros mismos."
—Carlos Fuentes, *Gringo Viejo*

The boundary was easy to cross. It still is. Despite all the efforts to enforce discipline on it, it remains chaotic. As population and economic pressures have mounted, its permeability has become an essential feature of North American geography. Without an ocean, mountain range, or other natural barrier, the line is entirely a human construct—a legalism laid across the land.
—William Langewieshe, *Cutting for Sign*

OUT OF THE FRYING PAN

For eighteen years, as I look back on it now, I had been letting the border get in the way of my seeing the desert from top to bottom, end to end, as one complete place. I don't know how I could've let myself do that. Somehow, we talk ourselves into slicing the land into pieces: as if cactus-fruit gathering, medicinal herbs, *cimarrónes*, desert varnish, *norteño* music, and crimson sunsets could be commonplace on one side but not on the other.

I suddenly realized that Brien Fiel was correct when he said that "civilization often follows a contour that no longer matches the landscape of fact." I had let that border become a barrier as much as the next guy had, forgetting that before the Gadsden Purchase most everyone knew southern Arizona and northern Sonora as one place: Pimería Alta.

What I needed was a new map for my head that had risen from my feet. I had to figure out a way to stitch what had seemed like a mess of frayed threads back into one cohesive fabric, like a big *serape* that could cover this arid region from head to toe. And so I took off on what my Arab kin call a *hadj*, a sacred expedition of two hundred miles, mostly on foot, from Sacaton, Arizona, to Magdalena, Sonora, a shrine in the heart of the desert that has been a spiritual magnet for centuries. Still, that shrine was not the place most people were looking for as a choice for their summer vacation. To get there, I would end up journeying eight days across desert ranges and valleys during what turned out to be the hottest summer on record—165 days with temperatures exceeding one hundred degrees.

The route I followed was the Sonoran Catholic pilgrim's trail to the shrine for San Francisco, a renegade saint who has lured O'odham, Yaqui, Hispanic, and Anglo-American peregrines alike. Saint Francis is probably not the one you have heard of elsewhere in the Christian world. This San Francisco is not necessarily from Assisi, nor the one that Jesuit missionaries first brought to this desert in the 1690s. Instead, this one wanders the desert alone. Down in Sonora, they tell how he has healed animals that he found injured and dying, and how he has sheltered and returned to safety young women violated by the troops of Pancho Villa.

I've heard tell that San Francisco can also make more summer rains come in time to save the crops and livestock. Because this saint has the wherewithal to bring the rains, my hunch is that most Sonorans only get around to paying him much attention when a drought has lasted far too long. Suffering through one such hellacious *sequía,* a Sonoran chicken farmer living out past Caborca toward the arid coast decided to try what his Mayo Indian wife had earlier urged him to do. He plopped a little statue of San Francisco out in his field of milo maize, right where he sorely wanted it to rain.

Nothing happened. His sorghum continued to wither. So he climbed up on the hot tin roof of his barn and mounted the statue up there where he could have full access to the sky. Still no rain came. A little hot under the collar—both at his wife and her "lazy Indian saint"—the frustrated farmer went up on the roof again, but this time he hung the statue upside down from the lightning rod. The instant he did, *relampagos* charged the sky with such force that the farmer could hardly get off the roof fast enough. The rains came, but as the farmer learned, San Francisco exacts a price. In this case a bolt of lightning missed the rod, soared down through the tallest mesquite post holding up the roof, cracking the post and sending it thundering down on top of the adobe wall. The electric charge itself singed the feathers off the hens roosting against the wall and killed the couple's last ornery old rooster.

When I began my pilgrimage in September thunderstorms had not touched the desert all summer long. I had been in metropolitan Phoenix, "an urban heat island," said the local weatherman, who blamed the record-high nighttime temperatures there on the asphalt and heat exhausts from air conditioners. Over the last forty years, he claimed, the maximum summer temperatures had risen four degrees, in perfect lock-step with urban sprawl.

I could feel this interminable heat and drought and see its effects on the wilted plants I had been trying to tend in my urban garden. The drought and scorching sun killed most of my seedlings, and the hungry varmints finished off the rest. I grew sick of Phoenix and sick of trying to keep a place green that was no longer suited to plant life. I could see no redeeming value in that forbidding city, even in its last few open spaces, like the nearly denuded Papago Park where I had been working.

So I fled Phoenix at four-thirty one September morning and gathered with a few friends in the dry riverbed of the Gila River twenty-five miles to the south. There, I began my pilgrimage while facing a cloudless lemon-colored sunrise. I had the good luck of convincing Adrian Hendricks that he should come at least part of the way with me. Adrian was a twenty-four-year-old O'odham runner, artist, and gardener whose biting comments could punctuate hours of silence. Lean, and a strong runner in the worst heat, Adrian had his own personal and cultural reasons for running, walking, and hobbling along with me for the first two days. Whatever they were, I was grateful for his company, especially when a dozen other friends told me that I was crazy for wanting to run the first twenty miles of a two-hundred-mile trek.

Adrian and I ignored their cautions, in part because we felt buoyed up by the help of other friends who were willing to move our packs ahead of us by car and supply us with food and bedding along the way. We were set on the right course by a young O'odham prayer leader, Culver Cassa, who had lived with my family for nearly a year before returning home to Sacaton.

When everyone had assembled, Culver took out a leafy branch from an exotic mulberry bush, dipped it in water, and blessed us. I had expected a traditional O'odham pilgrimage song and a creosote bush sprig, but instead, Culver read from Genesis 28. He read of wayfarers with no more than stones to place beneath their heads and tired bodies at night: "Behold, I am with you and this shall remain your land wherever you shall journey." Culver then added his own assurance: "Everything will be all right at home, so don't be filled with worry; just let your mind go straight to where your feet are going."

INTO THE FIRE

As the sun came up, our minds were released and we began to run. We ran away from the nearly dead Gila River, choked now with tamarisk sprouts introduced from the Middle East; we ran through the fallow fields that once made the Akimel O'od-ham the most prosperous farmers west of the Mississippi. We passed whitewashed Catholic chapels, abandoned Indian cars, tumbled-down mud-and-wattle houses, and mounds of tumbleweeds, all signs of a native life in transition. We ran close to five miles before Adrian steered me into a little *rincón* strewn with boulders. He broke his pace and nodded toward a cluster of giant granitic rocks that had the desert varnish scratched from their faces.

Horned toads, birds, and bighorns covered the rocks. Petroglyphs. Wavering spirals, river snakes, and mazes. Adrian then led me to another boulder, one with a cross mounted in a trinity, an arch of hammered-out dots—perhaps rosary beads—surrounding it. The date, 1763, was inscribed nearby, only seventy years after the first visit by missionaries; it was at a time when Old World diseases were decimating the O'odham, leaving them with hardly enough men to tend the fields.

Catching his breath, Adrian explained why he wanted me to see this place: "My grandfather and I used to come here on Sundays. I'd drive him over to Casa Grande for church, then we'd get some take-out food to bring here. We'd come and sit and look at those drawings. And now, my grandfather's dead, and I haven't come back to keep an eye on the place often enough."

He chugged the water in his canteen, then continued: "There's a new paved road nearby, so I guess the teenagers can get out here to party. One of them painted *God loves you* over the older drawings on the rock. The only thing I could think of when I saw it was this: He probably doesn't love you when you go and spray paint over these rocks. I guess all those kids want to get into it, like they think they're doing the same thing that the old ones did by leaving their marks here."

We ran another seven miles until our eyes burned with the salt from our sweat. We knelt down to drink from a crusty irrigation pipe, and the water spewing out of it was salty, mineralized groundwater pumped from the depths of the earth. A few months before, I had sat nearby with a Mexican friend and had roughed out the costs of these cultivated fields. When alfalfa and ryegrass are planted to raise feedlot beef, they use twenty tons of irrigation water to make one pound of hamburger. The groundwater around here has already dropped from twelve feet below ground level to more than two hundred since the 1920s.

A century ago, one manmade object as tall as the center pivot irrigation pipes and water towers stood out on these desert plains: Ge Ki, a prehistoric multistory ceremonial center, rose up from a mesquite forest. Today, the Indian ruin sits in Casa Grande National Monument, right in the middle of hundreds of acres of rotting trees killed by the drawdown of groundwater below their root level. What we have now is a National Park of Dead Stumps.

By midmorning, Adrian and I had each sweated away untold gallons of water. My thirst was not quenched by the mineralized tap water in the Casa Grande Valley. In desperation I turned to a low-sodium, filtered, chlorine-free, sanitized water vending machine. Before I figured out how to feed it a quarter to get my gallon of salt-free liquids, I had to read a panel full of instructions. Its main message was to forget local water because "ordinary tap water contains many impurities that not only attack you but even attack machines."

I reckoned that we hadn't actually seen any "local water" for the first twelve miles of our run. It was either imported from Rocky Mountain springs in the form of vending machines, from the Arizona highlands by way of huge diversion projects, or from the Ice Age in the form of fossil groundwater. Only the creosote bushes seemed to be getting along just fine on local rainfall alone; most everybody else, from farmers to feedlot calves, from cotton to tamarisks to tumbleweeds, seemed to be living on borrowed water.

The heat had climbed to 105 degrees when our pace downshifted from a run to a walk. Still, we had ten more miles to go before we would stumble into the first village on the Tohono O'odham Reservation. My head ached, and the dripping salt stung the skin covering my rib cage. I began to have doubts that I would see this desert journey through to "completion"—that is, to get a sense of the Sonoran Desert as something cohesive. The northern side of the line seemed so frayed: dry wells, denuded lands, abandoned houses with broken windows, gutted chassis of Ramblers and Edsels. It seemed as if all the junked cars, tractors, trailers, and mobile homes that had been ridden into the West since the Dust Bowl had come to a stop in the Casa Grande Valley. They were just waiting for another fiery blast of wind to come along and send them on their way once more.

We passed the Last Chance Gas and Booze market before crossing onto the "rez," as the locals still call the tribal lands of the O'odham nation. There, a Mexican migrant worker asked us where we were going, in between guzzles from his bottle of beer. "*Somos peregrinos, pues, estamos caminando para Magdalena, Sonora,*" I told him.

"*¡Hijole! Está muy lejo,*" he said, shaking his head to indicate that it was simply too far, and then he launched into a soliloquy about how lost we must be: "*Ustedes están bien norteado . . .*" He slurred his words, and Adrian could not understand him. I made him repeat what he was saying, but it was a jumble of fragments about how neither he nor anyone else should veer this far away from the protection of the saints. I gradually picked up the fact that he knew the shrine where we were headed and had stopped at it briefly on his way to the border by train. His people venerated Saint Francis. What people? I wondered. A few sentences later, he clarified: "*No soy Méxicano. Soy Indio Crudo, pero no soy Papago como los Indios aquí. Mi familia es de la tribu Cora. Somos de las sierras de Nayarit.*"

I had once seen a group of Cora Indians in costume. They had made a pilgrimage hundreds of miles by train to the shrine in Magdalena. There, they took to danc-ing, stepping in line to some curious songs—ancient-sounding but all in honor of Saint Francis. I asked this Cora farmworker how far people could be from the shrine and still be within the guidance of San Francisco. Did it, I wondered, have a range like the radio waves being emitted from some microwave tower on a mountaintop?

"*Pues, ¿quién sabe?*" he said, again shaking his head, still stupefied by the notion that we were trying to walk that far into Mexico. He moved away to swill his beer, moaning some old *corrido,* in a corner below the overhanging roof of the liquor store. I turned around and saw a few dark clouds coming toward us, too small to offer much rain. Soon they were pelting us with little BBs of water: I had been wrong.

Adrian nodded uncomfortably toward the clouds. "Maybe we wanted water too much. Well, now we got it," he mumbled. The rain soon quit, and as we limped along through more abandoned fields, I remembered what an O'odham elder—a farmer whom both Adrian and I knew—had told me once. His story underscored the O'od-ham belief that it was disrespectful to have an overzealous desire for water.

I was telling that elder what had happened to the chicken farmer in Caborca, when he grew pale. He told me that this Mexican had gotten off easy. He made me promise that I would never try such a stunt. He claimed that those who are too pushy in asking San Francisco for water must soon reckon with the *santu* in other ways:

"I remember my mother telling me about what he did back then when she was just married. She said it had sure been hot, and no rain had come for a long time, and all the grass had dried up so there was nothing for the cows. So she went into the chapel and got the *santu* and put him outside. She prayed real hard for rain for eight days straight and kept after him. Then on the ninth day, while she was praying, a storm came up out of nowhere. The rain began to beat down on her like someone had picked up a bucket of water and threw it at her. The raindrops bit at her skin. So she ran out to get the *santu* to bring him inside to stop it, but it kept on raining and raining. She started to get scared then: the water had begun to run across the ground, everywhere, in sheets, everywhere she looked the land had turned into rivers. To get him to stop, she had to stay inside and light every candle she had, and she had to keep on praying and praying until the rains went away again."

I realized that I was already getting weary from seeing so many wounded wildlands, eroded fields, and fallen-down homes. I wanted to know a desert that could soothe me out of my dirt-tired state of mind, but darkness was already falling. Adrian and I hobbled into the O'odham village of Ce:co Weco and found that our packs had been plunked down on the porch of Adrian's aunt. Within a half hour, we were asleep on that porch, surrounded by the vines of the bottle gourd, grown by the family to make ceremonial rattles. Those vines grounded me, and the sound of their rustling leaves kept me close to the earth as I floated through a night full of dreams.

BEYOND ANY ROAD

Half a night, really, for we crawled out of our sleeping bags just before three in the morning and took to the road by three-twenty. We had guessed that the coming day might take us across the longest waterless stretch we'd have to face, so we decided to do as much walking as we could in the cool of the night. While we walked from Ce:co Weco to White Horse Pass, I realized that the road was familiar. When I first moved to the desert, I had been taken to the village by an O'odham woman whose kinfolk came from here, though she had never mentioned the town's name. There, in the dark of the night, we looked over the sleeping body of the village I had first seen fifteen years before. I closed my eyes for a moment.

"There," she had nodded, "there is where my home rests." We looked out across the desert flats: a scatter of mud houses, set in place by the wind. Stretches of six-weeks grama grass lay dying in between them. As we walked toward their *va:tto*—an O'odham ramada, a bower of ocotillo ribs and cactus bones—we caught one scent of home: her mother cooking tortillas on the metal lid of a fifty-gallon drum suspended over a mesquite fire.

"I can smell my home, sometimes, from miles away," she had told me, inhaling. "Even before the rain brings its greasewood smell to my nose."

Adrian and I walked silently into the slumbering *ranchería*. In the hand-built chapel, we stopped a minute to pay our respects to the San Franciscito figure lying in repose. We shed a few expendable supplies that were weighing down our packs, then headed southward into a valley that had no name on our maps. Those maps told us something else, something more disturbing: we would probably not hit another *ranchería* for at least thirty miles.

While that piece of information alone could have put me on edge, something else had calmed me down. I finally found in the moonlight what I had been hurting for the day before: a kind of serenity in the country itself. It was unspoiled by ditches and doublewide trailers with satellite dishes. It was not yet spinning with center-pivot sprinklers. We found volcanic ridges and cobbly *bajadas,* thousands of cactus, ancient patches of creosote bush. And the legume trees—paloverde and mesquite and iron-wood—had big, full, uncut canopies. Canopies like halos, being backlit by moonbeams the way they were. Special breeds of strong, upstanding saints—those elderly statesmen of the desert—those paloverdes and creosotes and ironwoods and mesquites.

For several hours, we walked in silence, hearing only the sporadic calls of a great horned owl. No need for talk. Adrian and I kept plodding along the paths set out before us by the moonlight. We savored that fine unbroken stretch of nocturnal desert until twilight turned to dawn.

We snaked our way down into a valley that no paved road has ever entered; it was tucked somewhere between the Silverbells and the Silver Reef Mountains. There, we sat and ate a breakfast of hand-ground blue corn pinole that Adrian's Hopi girlfriend had given us. The native breadstuff warmed our bellies, and finally the sun broke over the horizon to warm our faces, legs, and hands.

That was when we decided to head south toward the long-abandoned village of Santa Ana de Kuivivulidag. An old teacher of mine, Bunny Fontana, had told me that it was the northernmost mission in the Sonoran Desert built during the colonial period. The Santan band of O'odham had left it decades before, moving up near the Gila River Indian Reservation where Adrian lives today. We knew many Santanners and wanted to see where they had come from. For a three-mile stretch that morning, we set our sights on a single tall tree on the southern horizon, crunching through bur sage and brittlebush, never seeming to reach the tree. Adrian looked weary for the first time, and the sun was already burning down on us. He grimaced and pulled his ball-cap visor down over his forehead.

"I think that tree has finally stopped running away from us," he offered, deadpan.

"No, it's still crawling southward. It doesn't want us to catch up."

I wondered if it could be a cottonwood tree or even a large mesquite because the Santanners had named their hometown after such a prominent tree. In the Pima or O'odham tongue, *kuivivulidag* means "[mesquite] tree tightened in the middle."

In this desert tongue, the words for *tree* and *mesquite* are the same. Another way of putting it is that mesquite represents the ultimate in what a tree can be to desert dwellers, just as cottonwood does for other Southwest Indians. Mesquites and cotton-woods loom larger than any other kind of life in the desert and can be seen from miles away. Where they grow, you know you have a lick of a chance of finding water, and maybe game as well. And in our case, after hours of hoofing across uninterrupted wild-lands, the sight of that tree might mean that we were coming close to the old mission ruins and its well, or to another, more recent settlement.

It turned out to be the latter, for we never found the Santan ruins. But for a half mile before we arrived at the tree and rejoined the humanized world, we could see a house, a cotton field, and a water tank. Still, they were surrounded by miles of desert scrub..

I was relieved: we wouldn't have to walk four to six more hours without enough water. We were down to a little more than a gallon and a half each, and we knew we'd need more than that for the rest of the day. It was not even eleven in the morning, but the temperature had already climbed way past one hundred degrees.

The tree was a joke on me: it was neither mesquite nor cottonwood, but euca-lyptus, imported from the Australian outback. The ranch house next to it was a mess, its windows broken, wasps in the walls, and century plants dead in the front yard. Still, there were signs of life: meat jerked on barbwire running across the front porch, and a dripping faucet, both buzzing with flies and honeybees. We drank and drank as the flies began to buzz all around us.

Someone sprang out from a small trailer on the side of the water tank. It was a Mexican ranch hand, confused and embarrassed by our presence.

"*¿Como se llama este rancho?*" I asked him, trying to figure out on my map where we were exactly in relation to the old mission ruins.

"*¡Fijate, no sé, amigo, porqué nadie ha preguntadome antes!*" he said, scratching his head.

"What does he call this place?" Adrian asked, wanting me to translate.

"He says he don't know. No one ever came out here and asked him before."

A rancher had simply put this hired hand out in that godforsaken trailer a year ago, brought him supplies once every two weeks, and instructed him to keep the cotton irrigated and the few head of cattle and horses alive. We knew we were just outside the reservation boundary, and that the only roads out here must lead east to Eloy, at least twenty miles away. If the ranch hand got bored or fed up with the living conditions out here, he'd have one hellacious walk or pony ride to get back into town. On top of that, he was probably considered by the government to be an "undocumented alien" or, as the Tex-Mex songs say, *un mojado sin licencia.* He had been left out in the boonies by a rancher who could turn him in to *la migra* if he tried to complain.

Funny thing was, the ranch hand was as worried about us as we were about him. "*¿Van para Magdalena por pie?*" he asked, spitting some tobacco out away from us. "*Pues, no hay camino. Desde aquí, se chingó el camino.*"

"He says that there ain't no road that can get us from here to Magdalena. He says from here, the road is all chingered up. He says that we're either lost or out of our minds."

Taking pity on us, I suppose, the *vaquero* asked if we wanted to stay and work with him until his boss showed up, rather than running ourselves into the ground. I translated this to Adrian, too, who looked around at all the crap in the yard and said, "No way; let's get outa here."

I took one last look: the kicked-in plasterboard of the ranch house walls, the dead refrigerator, the sardine cans heaped up on the porch, the three hoes hooked into the paneless window jamb. Failed attempts at converting the desert always look their worst when they're still surrounded by wildness. We took one last drink from the faucet, thanked our host for the water, the offer, and the talk. We walked on.

That ranch hand was right about one thing, though. The route we wanted to follow was as clogged as any route could get. I am not whining when I declare that afternoon the toughest of the entire trip. As we tried to follow one wash after another, we must have walked five miles out of our way—assuming that we had one—and then we got lost on top of that. We were tangled up in a huge mesquite forest where dozens of arroyos braided together, then diverged. At dusk, when I was too wasted to even climb a barbwire fence, Adrian hoisted himself up to the top of a windmill and spotted a light to the southeast of us.

"I see some light we can head for—let's hope it's over at Queen's Well," Adrian yelled down to me, the weariness carrying in his voice. "That's where I told my mother and Brenda that we would meet them at five tonight." It was already seven. The thought of them waiting there helped him to muster up another burst of energy. His tenacity in seeking out that light carried me along too.

We were back on reservation land, land that had been heavily grazed at one time and heavily eroded since. In the dark, we climbed up and down, in and out of ten-foot-deep gullies, stubbing our toes, sliding, tripping over roots, waiting for the moon to shed some light on a path, any path that we could follow. My feet ached up to my hips.

At nine-fifteen—eighteen hours after we had started walking that day—we stumbled up to a house with a light on inside. I knocked on the door. A middle-aged O'odham man answered.

"Are we anywhere near the Queen's Well feast house?"

"No, not really . . ."

I shot a worried glance at Adrian. The man continued his sentence, slowly.

"No, you have to go about four more buildings down . . ."

Within minutes, we saw two women pacing inside the open feast house door. Adrian broke stride and lunged into the arms of his fiancée, Brenda, and his mother from Sacaton.

Sacaton. It was not even two days since we left the Gila River at dawn. Sixty miles and many stories later, we fell asleep on the feast house floor.

STITCHING TOGETHER ANCIENT THREADS

"I knew you would have trouble coming through those arroyos," the widow Angelita said to me the next morning as she brought me a cup of coffee. Adrian and his family had already driven away in his pickup. "Sure a lot of little mesquites over there. Not now, but a long time ago, there were just a few big trees and lots of grass up there. You could see a long way without any trouble." She stirred fresh green corn in with the summer squash and chiles in her frying pan and handed me a large wheat tortilla.

"I didn't see much grass up there. *Pi 'o sa'i*," I repeated in O'odham, for I knew she liked to hear me try out my rudimentary knowledge of her mother tongue. I had known Angelita Enriquez and her sons for nearly twelve years.

"No, ever since those missionaries brought us all those cows and horses, they have been eating all the grass. They carry the mesquite seeds up from the washes and drop them there, and we get our *kui kuagi*—our firewood—where the grasses once grew."

"When did the missionaries come here?" I asked, assuming that she was referring to Padre Kino or to the later Spanish Franciscans. Then I realized that she was speaking of the American Franciscans who arrived around the turn of the century, after the O'odham had already been adapting Catholicism to their own culture over the previous century and a half.

"My mother was the first baptized Catholic in the central part of our country. I don't know what year. She told me that Father Mattia just walked into their bean field one day and asked if there was any place where he could say Mass. So they took him over to our *uksa*—you know, our outdoor kitchen with walls just made of brush. He set up his things in that *uksa* and baptized her right then and there.

"Not long after that, my mother lived for a while over in Comobabi, where the old people were afraid of becoming American Catholic. They still held on to their old beliefs. That was when my mother had to explain to one old man that Saint Francis was not God. 'There's God-the-Father-in-Heaven,' she explained, 'and then there's God-the-Son-in-Jesus-Christ. You understand, old man?' Well, that old man just looks at her, nodding and blinking. Finally, he says something: 'Well, yes, there are two of them, I guess: that Saint Francis must be the Father and Jesus his Son.'

"I haven't been to Magdalena since I was first married," she said, holding my hand, realizing that I would soon be going. "I went by wagon that one time, and I didn't like it for the drinking. My husband bought some tequila. My lips burned. I wanted to leave. But later, I remember when the Mexican government tried to stop our fiesta. They took Saint Francis away to the state capital in Hermosillo. When our people, the O'odham, arrived in Magdalena anyway, they couldn't find him anywhere at first. But they kept looking and praying for him. Finally, they say, they learned he had escaped and came back on the train to see them."

Her son José, seeing me limping with bruised and blistered feet, offered to drive me to the trailhead of a shortcut to the next village; he said I wouldn't be able to find it on my own. I accepted, and for ten minutes we bounced along in his low-riding Ford on an old wagon trail hidden among all the desert growth. He talked about the time when he and his brother and I had tried to fix up his father's abandoned field, but the rains hadn't sustained the store-bought seeds he had planted there.

"That was when you suggested that I plant some of the old-style seeds from my people," he said, sadly. "I should have known to do that anyway. Now I understand that those old seeds can withstand the weather. I'm beginning to see all the ways the past can help us even now, how the ancient songs should be learned even by my daughter to guide her through the rest of her life. It's good what we got started here. Come around again sometime, and I'll show you what I'm up to."

José left me on my own, four miles or so from San Pedro village, and I hobbled along. My feet had become tender, and my heart was not much better off. Fortunately, the ground was soft, for the trail was close enough to Kitt Peak to have received rain recently, but out of sight of any roads. I had a couple hours to plod along by myself across a desert grassland that seemed as though it had not been ravaged by drought. At last, there were grasses in flower and seed: gramas, cottontops, bluestems, and three-awns. They were tucked up between mesquites and Mormon teas, prickly pears, barrels, and five different kinds of cholla cactus. It was midday, yet no one had yet slunk off for a siesta: coyotes howled, caracaras soared overhead, and even a heron flew up from the muddy floor of a little water hole. It was hard to feel alone. A world was buzzing wildly around me.

That feeling did not stop when I arrived in San Pedro village. There, Frances Manual, an O'odham matriarch, had a modest feast prepared on my behalf. As she hugged me, I realized how compact she was relative to the image of her I had kept in my mind: an elderly but big-boned woman whose long hair was always piled high and elegantly pinned, whose simply spoken stories could conjure up huge mythic scenes in front of my eyes. But before she called to the other houses to have her neighbors come over, she took me aside and talked to me alone.

"By coming through our village like this, you are reminding us to do what our parents taught us to do," she began solemnly. "When I was a little girl, I remember that when someone walked through on their way to Magdalena, everyone would come up to him, shake his hand, offer him something to drink, and send their prayers with him. Saint Francis is my *tocayo,* my namesake; the birds are his friends, the wilderness his home. That's how it is for me too."

She told me of the time when the people were first introduced to Francis, a time when they still didn't accept him as a saint. He had built a church for them, but they never went inside. Frances leaned toward me:

"Then one day an earthquake came. It scared the pigeons as it began to shake, and so they came to the church and nested down within it. Even the donkeys came and took refuge, but the people still did not see what was going on. Finally, all of their houses were falling down, and even the church was rocking and wavering like it was going to break," she said, waving her hand back and forth like a quivering wall.

"Suddenly, the pigeons came out, and their wings had become harps. The donkeys began to honk and honk, and their sound became a song about Saint Francis," and she sang, in Spanish, a few verses of their song. Her voice warbled with a delicacy that I had not expected. "That is when the people realized that they needed to be part of it—what we call the Santu Himdag—or everything would fall down. That is when they all went running to the fold, you know, just like they did 'long time ago in that other desert. You know, that time when Jesus brought the fish . . ."

I was there with her, in that ancient desert where stories thrive.

The neighbors had all gathered outside in a circle, bringing food along with them. A friend from Phoenix, Chris Keith, had arrived to check up on me. We all chatted for a while as Lorenzo unwrapped his gourd rattle, and then grew silent as he began a song in O'odham.

Frances had prepared a short oration: "*Hegai* Gary—some of you know him—he is walking through from Akimel O'odham Ha-Jewed [Pimaland] up there on the Gila River, clear down to Ma'lina [Magdalena]. We are glad that he is reminding us what our own people have done for a long time. When I was small, my grandmother would call me whenever she saw a pilgrim entering our village. She would tell me to go ahead and get some things ready for him. She would talk to me, saying that just because he was dirty, or sweaty or ugly, don't judge him by his looks, but by what he is doing. Bring him water and some food and help him on his way."

I looked down at the mud on my shorts, the holes in my shoes, the scratches on my calves, the bandanna around my neck soaking with sweat. I had become one of those dirty, sweaty, ugly ones for sure.

One of the women from the village giggled. "When we saw him walking into town a little while ago, we thought he was a wetback who was going the wrong way." Then she came and gently hugged me. Others followed.

We all shared in food, small talk, and drink, then Frances took me out to her fence to send me on my way. "When you get down into Mexico, remember me. Part of me is from that land. I've never told many people, but I guess I can tell you: I'm not full-blood O'odham; I'm part Mexican and Seri Indian too."

"Seri?" I repeated, surprised that I had not noticed how tall she was, how her bone structure was not like that of her O'odham neighbors.

"It's on my mother's side—she was half Mexican, because her father was Antonio Lopez. His wife was Seri—they called her Xu:d." *Xu:d*, I knew, is a word layered with meanings. In one context, it may mean "puddle"; in another, it may refer to a coffee cup or even a woman "full to the brim."

My throat was real dry. "I'll carry your thoughts to Ma'lina and to your namesake, Saint Francis." A touch of our hands, and I was off.

Even though my mangled feet had made me limp through the morning, I was suddenly running again. Running with just a small hip pack on over my shorts, for Chris had offered to drive my other gear farther along down the road. Running down a dirt track from the village, and out onto the first asphalt I had seen for nearly fifty miles. Running, suddenly, with a drive that seemed to void any difficulties the blisters and bruises had given me. I caught glimpses of oystercatchers and vultures taking flight up from the little rain-fed water holes nearby. The dark and brittle ground was still beneath my feet, but it was no longer a constraint. I soared.

I ran miles—several more miles—down the highway into Avra Valley toward

Brawley Wash, east toward Tucson. I ran at full steam until I was derailed: my thigh muscles locked up on me. In a second, I was down on the side of the road, massaging a hard pain in my leg with my fists, unable to walk or run.

I had been buoyed by an endorphin high, and by the sweetness of my O'odham friends. Now I was down in the gutter, next to a roadside shrine, where an O'odham unknown to me had been killed in a car accident years ago. As I tried to rub the knots out of my thighs, I glanced over at the empty Camel cigarette packs and Cuervo tequila bottles filling the niche of the shrine. Neither would help me much now.

I watched a car full of O'odham kids and adults drive past, drift down through the watery mirages that splashed across the highway, and then I went back to seeing if there was any way that massage could help my vapor-locked thighs. The next time I looked up, there was José Enriquez once again; it was the same car that had driven us out to the trailhead earlier that morning.

"Let me help you in," he said, as I hopped, one-legged, over to the car. "We were just driving along, but I had this feeling I might see you out here."

"Just look where the vultures are circling," I moaned, laughing, but then I closed my eyes and let them drive me down to the Three Points Trading Post where other friends would find me shelter for the night.

FINDING MORE FRAYED THREADS

That evening I slept on a cot in the backyard of my *compadre,* Tom Sheridan. He was the one who had introduced me to Sonoran fever in the first place, hauling me down to a Magdalena fiesta a dozen years before. As I stretched out on the handmade Sonoran cot, Tomás caught a glimpse of the bottoms of my feet, blisters like cumulonimbus clouds rising before a summer storm. "Hey, Nabhan, you got some troubles ahead with your toenails."

I looked down at them. Purple blood blisters had formed beneath them. Nothing new, I mumbled; it has happened before when I've run too far in too short a time.

"Nabhan, I'm telling you, I think your toenails are gonna pop off. You have a good pocket? You're gonna hafta carry them with you to Saint Francis."

I hadn't been able to hold down any food that night, but it didn't seem to matter much. I simply slept outside beneath the stars, and whenever the muscle cramps woke me up, I drank some Gatorade and tried to sleep again.

The next morning, I headed cross-country for Ryan Field, a little airstrip just past the outskirts of Tucson. From there, I veered south toward the Yaqui Indian village of New Pascua. I was in the mood to grieve a little: conceding the present miserable condition of my feet, noticing the equally miserable condition of the desert around me— a choke of stinking lovegrass and South African buffelgrass, tumbleweeds, and Bermuda. Alien weeds lined the ditches, infested the washes, and covered the abandoned fields. Next to the clutter of these seedy, exotic plants, I was hardly bothered by the scatter of plastic bags, spewed-out cassette tapes, cigarette packets, and Bud Light cans. Hell, trash could decompose, rust, or be carried off to birds' nests and packrat heaps over the next decade. But I'd be looking at tumbleweeds and other noxious introductions from here all the way to the end of my *hadj*.

I entered the Yaqui village on the ragged edges of metropolitan Tucson. The Yaqui too were newcomers here in the sense that about a century ago, they fled from their ancestral homeland hundreds of miles south in the southern Sonoran Desert. And yet, they have made some kind of accommodation to *this* place, at the same time that they kept up ties to their *patria*. What made them behave as natives to the desert in ways that other newcomers did not? It was never so simple as calling one group Native Americans and another foreigners.

I noticed a wreath made of Fremont cottonwood leaves blessing the door of a Yaqui household. It was not the same kind of cottonwood that lined the banks of the Río Yaqui, but it served a kindred purpose here. Crosses carved out of mesquite circled their plaza. Live cottonwoods and paloverdes provided shade around the ceremonial grounds. White-winged doves nested in the rafters of their chapel. A few young men with long hair tucked beneath their palm sombreros were cleaning wind-deposited debris from the plaza and pruning the trees. There was a homegrown community spirit here—still intact—that didn't seem overwhelmed by the newly constructed subdivisions all around their funky homes. I lumbered through those tidy subdivisions to reach the Mission San Xaviér.

On the other side of the developers' instant neighborhoods, my old friends Tom Orum and Nancy Ferguson housed me on their ancient farmland along Los Reales road. They brought me a tub so that I could soak my blistered feet, then talked me into bicycling rather than walking the next leg of my journey. We talked about the huge garden patches they tend behind their trailer and their work away from home. Tom had recently been out crawling around looking for baby saguaros under paloverdes. He was rereading some old cactus study plots established decades ago, trying to figure out whether saguaros were increasing or declining in number. Nancy, in turn, had been out following around twenty-eight radio-tagged desert tortoises through the Tucson Mountains.

"Aside from the esoteric benefits to science," she said dryly, "I'm personally getting to know two of those little guys pretty well on a week-to-week basis." Nancy explained how she had tracked one female over an area that was a mile and a half in diameter, but then lost her at the start of the winter, for the "Lady of the Rock" had not returned to her cave. The tortoise had decided instead to sleep under a dead saguaro all winter beyond the range where Nancy had been hunting. Nancy was jubilant when she reencountered the Lady the following spring. "But I worry about her crossing roads and getting run over. As far as these tortoises go, they need all the extra uninvaded space we can give them."

WEAVING IN RESILIENCE

Next morning, I had breakfast with Big Jim Griffith, a banjo-playing, tall-tale-telling folklorist who lives on the edge of San Xaviér. Also big is the mole on his face that moves as he tells stories. He collects everything from Tex-Mex records to gravestone rubbings to bilingual borderland jokes, lending him a reputation as a huge and wacky walking encyclopedia of vernacular borderlands history. He wanted to talk with me about the "sacred geography" of the Sonoran Desert homeland—and did so while whipping us up a "kitchen-sink" version of *chilaquiles* in an oversized frying pan. At the same time, he told stories he had heard about Saint Francis from O'odham and Mexican friends:

How, when Plutarco Elías Calles was president, the Mexican government closed down the Magdalena fiesta in 1934. All they did, really, was trigger another miracle—the ancient carving of the saint reappeared in the middle of the desert, in the ground beneath Cuwi Ge:sk, "Jackrabbit-Falls-Down," now called San Francisquito, Sonora.

How the O'odham from S-cuculik, "Sure-a-Lot-of-Chickens-Around-Here," wanted to have a new carving of Saint Francis blessed by the old one in Magdalena. So they sat the two head-to-toe next to each other and left them alone in the room of the shrine. When they peeked in on them later, well, the two statues were sitting up, talking to each other, face-to-face.

And how a twelve-year-old Mexican girl was once kidnapped by soldiers who left her out in the desert, lost, until an old man came along on a donkey and rescued her. When he returned her to her parents and went into their chapel to pray, they noticed he had stickers all over his brown robe and wounds on his hands and feet. As he wandered away singing, they realized that the homely old man was none other than San Francisco.

For over an hour, Jim and I whipped stories back and forth across the table at each other. We slowly finished up his massive breakfast of stewed-and-brewed-together leftovers. Then, suddenly, he smacked his forehead and put his head down into the palms of his giant hands.

"Oh, hell, I forgot to tell you Julio called," Jim moaned. "He says he'll meet you at Martinez Hill before noon. Oh, and Nicholas Bleser called the other day, too, and hopes that you can get down to Tumacácori by tomorrow night. And I hear Susan Spater will be waiting for you in Nogales."

I suddenly understood that the word had gotten around, and the friends who were sheltering me along the way were prepping one another, making sure I was on time and okay.

I decided it was time to get on the bike that Tom and Nancy had been guarding for me, so I could wheel on over to find out where Julio was. On the way, I stopped in at the San Xaviér District office to talk with Daniel Preston. Danny's as big as Jim, and a warmhearted O'odham who has become a savvy community activist. When I stepped in his door, I could see he was flustered. I asked him if any trouble was in the air.

"Oh, it's nothin'. I just received a phone call from the Bureau of Rec staff—they wanted to move twenty saguaro cacti from 'their' right-of-way across Indian lands." Danny is as skeptical as I am. A good percentage of saguaros that get uprooted then plopped back down in the ground look okay for a year or two but then die a slow death from infections in wounds suffered during the transplant.

He argued that the Bureau of Reclamation should turn the issue inside out: for once, he'd like its staff to consider moving their operations out of the way of two-hundred-year-old plants. Their ancient roots deserved to be left in place.

"I guess I worry about them because those desert plants are a lot like we are. If you take us O'odham out of this environment, out of our earth, what we call O'od-ham Ha-Jewed, something about us is going to die too."

Here was a young guy who had to spend his time in a double-wide trailer-turned-office, talking to a bunch of bureaucrats on the phone, and he still spoke with wisdom, vision, humility toward others. The man was rooted, even though his office looked as if it had been wheeled in only a few minutes before.

Danny reminded me of the words of Alfredo Vea, Jr., a former migrant farm-worker from Arizona: "I used to think the Indians out here were powerless, but they're not, far from it. They just refuse to join up, that's all, and that is a very great strength. They have the power to remain themselves. They're the only ones who seem to see that so much of the white man's work is not progress."

I pedaled from Danny's trailer another mile past empty fields full of sinkholes, and crossed the now-dry riverbed of the Río Santa Cruz. There, Julio Betancourt greeted me, his long raven-black hair blowing in the hot breeze rising up the volcanic ridge where he stood. He kidded me about my limp, then guided me up an old trail from the Indian Health Clinic buildings at the base of Martinez Hill.

Julio goes after the history of any place he is working in like some fanatic detective, always unearthing tracks that no one else has ever noticed. Lately, Julio had been trailing the culprits who had turned a living river into a downcut gully—by culprits, I mean everyone from the infamous El Niño to cowboys, ditchdiggers, developers, and serendipity.

The Río Santa Cruz was once a river you could ferry down many Sundays out of the year, starting from the border near Nogales and Calabazas, floating northward until you ended up in Tucson, where you could have yourself a meal of freshwater clams and fish harvested there that day. But it had gone dry through an odd combination of human blunders and raging floods that hadn't been well understood. Enter detective Julio.

When a big flood last century ripped through the desert, the river had already been waiting like a loaded gun for some time. It may have been loaded, some say, when the Jesuit *padres* brought in the *criollo corriente* cattle to the watershed in the 1690s, stock that could consume both shrubby cover and grass with equal ease. Instead of sticking to generalities, Julio scoured old Spanish, Indian, and Anglo records for particulars that told him blow by blow, the pulling of the trigger inch by inch.

Julio carried me back to the Spring Branch of the Río Santa Cruz in 1849: "Back in those days, there was a *ciénaga* as big as a section of land down there," he said, pointing to the whereabouts of the six-hundred-some acres that once held marshy growth—all dead mesquite stumps and abandoned fields today. "There was a big mesquite *bosque* to the north of there too."

I tried to remember what some explorers' journals from the 1850s had said about the wildlife that this gallery forest attracted. "The Forty-Niners claimed that there were even Mexican wolves and grizzlies down here on the floodplain in the old days. And wasn't there a little mesquite mouse that's now extinct?"

"Well, the area under mesquite might have grown after the *ciénaga* marshlands were drained. But back in 1849, floodplain forest, wet meadows, and marshland were all intact, probably full of wildlife. That was about when a farmer named Jésus Maria Martinez got a little land grant from the Mexican government that made him neighbor to the O'odham at San Xaviér. The O'odham tolerated his presence as long as he wouldn't take water from the Spring Branch. So he dug a ditch on the floodplain at a spot called Punta de Agua. It's on the southwest side of the Santa Cruz Valley—over where the course of the river was before 1910, not the channel there below."

Julio stopped for a second and took a drink from my canteen. "Well, Martinez and the Indians used his ditch to draw on a real reliable source of water down at Box Spring. But the ditch Martinez dug ended up creating an incised channel, with a head-cut that interrupted the water table. Punta de Agua began to entrench early, perhaps earlier than most other arroyos in these parts. By the late 1850s, there was already a good-sized arroyo forming at Punta de Agua."

"Wouldn't the farmers have had trouble irrigating their beans and corn off his ditch?"

"They were still okay over at the Spring Branch, but it got bad over near Punta de Agua."

"So not all of them irrigated off his ditch?"

"No, the Indians wouldn't let him use the Spring Branch waters at all. Maybe because of what had happened over at the main channel, I'm not sure. But by 1871, a surveyor named Foreman recorded that an arroyo was already making its way upstream to the Spring Branch, having created a deep gash all the way from Valencia Road, four miles to the north. Down there, you suddenly had a gash with vertical banks ten feet deep, sixty feet from one to the next."

Palms at the site of an abandoned hacienda, Tempe

Desert cleared and waiting for water, near Tonopah

Coyote crossing near I-10

"Target Rd.," north of Gila Bend

Tow target, Barry M. Goldwater Bombing Range

Gas station off I-17, Black Canyon City

"A gash? A gully where it had been this marshy, slow-moving river?"

"Yeah, and by 1882, the next cut had gone twenty feet deep and water was bubbling out of it. They had intercepted the underflow for sure."

"You mean they were losing the groundwater? The springs that the farmers had been using for centuries?"

"That's right. Downstream at Tucson, however, the Santa Cruz was okay. One guy called it a mere brook with grassy banks. Then in the early 1880s, some farmers started clearing new lands to grow vegetables that used even more water than grain crops did. All of a sudden, there was this conflict between them and the more traditional farmers with lands above Saint Mary's Road."

"If they had traditionally grown Sonoran wheat, club barley, or tepary beans, they probably didn't need all that much water before."

"Yeah, but they switched. That dispute went to the county courts. The courts decided that the new farmlands to the north should remain fallow unless—or until—the near-surface underflow could somehow be tapped to increase the water supply."

"Uh-oh . . ."

"Yeah, that's when the shit hit. A Welshman named Sam Hughes shows up and builds an intercept ditch that taps the underflow near Saint Mary's crossing. Sometime late in 1888, he starts excavating a twenty-foot-wide ditch he wants to run for fifteen miles—that's the beginnings of what Tucson now knows as its 'Flowing Wells' district. Pretty soon, he just lets the floods of the following summer do the rest of the excavation."

"You mean all the water that reached him at Saint Mary's he shot straight downstream to cut a canal? Didn't he have a clue? Wouldn't it cut even worse if the force of a big flood came along?"

"He didn't have to wait too long before that very thing happened," Julio said with a grin. "On October 16, 1889, Hughes's neighbor Henry Buehman walked out his door with a camera and took a picture of what looked like a minor flood down at the Saint Mary's Road crossing. As he stood there, floodwaters cascaded into the eroded heading of Hughes's ditch and began the headcut, the one that eventually ruined much of the rest of the Santa Cruz floodplain."

"Julio, last time we talked you told me that the big floods in 1889 and 1890 may have been caused by El Niño storms. Didn't they arrive here sometime in the 1880s? I guess I don't know what you're saying about that. That some global climate change caused the arroyo cutting all over the Southwest, and not these silly ditches and the overgrazing that preceded them all over the region?"

"Well, look at the next arroyo-cutting storm that came along: in July and August of 1890, San Xaviér and Tucson received twelve inches of rainfall—about the average annual rainfall, all dumped in just two months. That's El Niño. You can't explain the floods that followed as results of only overgrazing, as if nothing slowed the water flows. Twelve inches in two months would have caused massive erosion even in prehistoric times, even before there were cows or ditchdiggers here."

"But those El Niño floods just before the turn of the century found nick points caused by human disturbances—little wounds to open into walloping holes."

"That's it. The 1891 floods eroded through the Silver Lake impoundment dammed by Rowlett in 1857. The 1894 floods eroded the channel at Ajo Way. By 1905, the floods hit Martinez Hill and threatened the Spring Branch. By 1910, the head-cuts on the two branches of the Santa Cruz joined at Valencia Road and could be seen below us here at Martinez Hill."

"Each one of those big floods may have been from an El Niño downpour, just like the one we witnessed here in October 1983?"

"El Niño, El Chubasco, El Arroyo—they've been called by different names at different times, but they've caused all the major floods of the last century."

"How did the people deal with them?" I wondered. "I mean, it left most of the farmers' fields high and dry."

"Well, early in this century, the Anglos in Tucson started pumping groundwater for irrigation. They eventually got their hands on the water by San Xaviér, too, and put in a well field down near the Indian reservation which we're still dependent on."

"First the springs the O'odham had used for centuries got taken and ruined, then the groundwater under their lands got taken and ruined."

Julio scratched his beard, looked out over the valley, then said, "For whom? For those land and water developers in Tucson, this arroyo cutting and aquifer depletion was just a technological problem, that's all. But for the O'odham at San Xaviér, it was a life problem. A real life problem."

REWORKING THE LOOM

There was a dust devil rising up in front of Martinez Hill as I left the O'odham lands at San Xaviér. The few leveled fields, still relatively clear of shrubs, were fallow this year, supporting nothing but pigweeds and thistles. These are the fields of an ancient agricultural folk Edgar Anderson once called "one of the world's most remarkable agricultural civilizations . . . they produce a usable harvest on fewer inches of rainfall than are used anywhere else in the world." Except where Danny's friend Clifford Pablo keeps up a small field of native crops, such seeds are all but gone from the Santa Cruz floodplain. So is the mesquite mouse and thirty-nine kinds of birds.

South of San Xaviér, the channels of the Santa Cruz form an eroded maze on *mal pais,* or "maul pies" as Anglo ranchers mangle the term. Badlands. Gullied arroyos with eight-foot-tall walls that look like eroding pillars of clay. Only cactus, tumbleweeds, and dwarf salt cedars try to hold them intact. Once a fertile floodplain, it had sure enough turned into something more akin to a mauled pie.

I crossed what is labeled a "Foreign Trade Zone" on the southeast edge of the Indian reservation. What hadn't been eroded away was being built over, covered up with asphalt and concrete. Factories, bingo casinos, discount cigarette stores, the whole nine yards. A curious little sign caught my eye on a chain-link fence surrounding a fairly dangerous looking electrical power transformer: "*S-ta E:bidama S-gewk 'O G Wepegi. Peligro: Voltaje Alto.* Danger. High Voltage."

A trilingual welcome to the world of perils.

It was just a few miles south down the road that I spotted a haven within all that waste. God's Little Acres, it was called. Someone's hands had restored color and life to a desolate place, using anything that washed into the neighborhood as building materials. It was a Mission-style cottage with walls lined with creek-washed cobblestones and pebbles. And all around it, covered with mosaics of more cobbles, pebbles, and blue inlaid glass shards, were miniature castles, thrones, doghouses, wishing wells, and sculptures of women, flowers, and mandalas. Above a porch made of wagon wheels, I saw the imprints of two tiny hands in concrete, with "Della, 1966" scrawled beside them. I parked my old five-speed and knocked on doors until I finally found a neighbor who knew Della's identity.

"Della? Della Wilcox? Well, she was sorta a borderline fool, but I kinda liked her. Died about four or five years ago, and the place has got run-down since then. But she built this wooden house and then put the rock around it like another layer of veneer. She was fixing to charge admission to folks to come in and see all her antiques and sculptures and such but just never got around to it."

"Did she do all this by herself?"

"After her husband died, she'd have one suitor after another show up, but she'd send 'em right back out into the desert, looking for wagon wheels so's she could build more things. Musta been a trail right through these parts, cuz they was always finding wheels they supposed came from covered wagons. Yeah, back then, there was enough water to lure folks along that there river behind us."

This guy had a good imagination, too, to still assume that the gully out behind his house was a river.

I got back on the road, glad I was on a bike instead of on foot. The pressure of my feet against the pedals was all I could bear, and the desert (or lack of it) was getting on my nerves. As I whizzed as fast as I could through the pecan groves south of Pima Mine Road, I recalled that at one time, this swath of irrigated nuts used more water than all the citizens of Tucson put together, forty million cubic yards a year.

Until recently, the Green Valley orchards were paradise for two of the most hostile mosquitoes that reach the borderlands. They would breed and feed in incredible numbers. For them, puddles beneath thirty-foot-tall pecans were probably even better habitat than the old mesquite forests and marshlands of the Santa Cruz.

If you stood still a moment in the shade of a pecan tree, you'd be lucky if any less than fifty mosquitoes went for your blood within a minute's time. A buddy of mine from years ago, naturalist Ken Kingsley, has only words of admiration for those floodwater mosquitoes: "They're migratory, attack in swarms, and are fierce, persistent, noisy, and painful biters."

With Ken's help, Green Valley later got free of its mosquito problem, just as it has with wind-battered trash, snotty-nosed kids, shade-tree mechanics, funky garden fences, and horse corrals made of junked cars stood on end. As one of Arizona's largest planned retirement communities, it seems flawless in ways that gave me the spooks.

I glided down its streets, dazzled by its lily-white stuccoed walls, manicured yards, and innumerable statues of St. Francis-of-the-Birdbath. Only trouble was, San Francisco had none of the birdshit on his shoulder that has become his signature of authenticity. The poor guy probably gets scrubbed down every morning here by blue-haired women with wire brushes.

Not far beyond Green Valley, I noticed a Mexican-American farmworker cutting pigweeds. He was back a ways from the road, in a ditch that ran between a field and a place where a mess of pecan trees had been chopped down and windrowed.

"*Hombre ¿'sta cosechando quelites pa' comer?*" I called, wondering if he'd be eating the greens he was clearing out of the ditch.

He looked at me intently, then stood up and stretched, arching his back. "No way, man. I get my greens someplace else. If you pick them from fields and orchards around here, who knows? You may get poisoned. You get rashes from the herbicides and insecticides just from walking through these weeds."

A couple miles north of the Canoa Ranch Road, the pecans finally stopped for good. Pumping the water table down for them seemed to have taken its toll on the cottonwood trees surrounding the old Canoa homestead: they were nearly all dead.

Down by Amado, I spotted the first roadside shrine I had seen since my leg had cramped up on the O'odham Reservation. This one had been done up by Mexicans rather than O'odham. It was jam-packed with candles and rosaries and paintings of saints rather than the booze, beans, and cactus syrup that O'odham victims of car accidents are fed so they can continue along after they die.

It was late in the afternoon now, and I was half dead, ready for someone to start making me my own roadside shrine. Even riding a bike had begun to wear hard on my feet and legs. I took the Nogales Highway access road down to Tubac, an old Spanish presidio that had been renovated as an artist's colony of late. I skipped through town as fast I could, beelining for the Santa Cruz where a cottonwood grove still hangs on. There, for the first time in over a hundred miles and four days, I saw a running river!

I dumped the bike, pulled my shoes off, and hobbled over to the flow. The Santa Cruz ran three to six feet wide, and four to six inches deep. As my feet sank into the mud, sand, and cobbles, and a cold rush of water rose to my ankles, I felt the same mix of pleasure and pain that hits me, well, when eating spicy hot food or having sex in a cramped setting. My feet didn't know whether to jump out of the water or to scream for more.

Without getting stark naked, I tried to give myself a good washing, rinsing my sweat-caked hair and scrubbing the bike-chain grease off my calves. If any of the Tubac elders had ridden down to the river then, I might have reminded them of the following notice written last century when the *Weekly Arizonan* was printed in Tubac (it was the first newspaper in the Sonoran Desert region): "*UGLY VISITORS.*—One night last week three bear, probably of the cinnamon species, came down and drank out of the Santa Cruz, within a few hundred yards of Tubac. The next morning they were seen on the trail to Santa Rita by a Mexican, who prudently rode around them and passed on."

A few miles down the road is Tumacácori Mission, where my friend Nicholas Bleser served as ranger-historian for the National Park Service. Nick loves to tell the story of the mission's curious origins. Built first by the Jesuits around 1753, the deteriorating mission had to be erected a second time between 1802 and 1828 by Franciscans. It is also one of the few national monuments in the United States that had to be established twice.

After the mission lands were donated by the Méndez family, Teddy Roosevelt brought Tumacácori into federal ownership in 1908. Six years later, the Supreme Court recognized that New Mexico's Baca family had a prior claim. In 1917 the Baca family returned the land to the government, and in December 1918, "Boss" Pinkley became Tumacácori's first custodian.

Even before Pinkley's arrival, there were observers who recorded activities around the mission, including Lieutenant Cave Couts, who traveled through Tumacácori just before the mission settlement was abandoned in 1848 because of constant raiding by the Apaches. At the time, most of its two dozen O'odham residents were away, celebrating the San Francisco "jubilee" down at Magdalena, Sonora:

"The churches in this valley are remarkable. At Tumacácori is a very large and fine church standing in the midst of a few conical Indian huts, made of bushes thatched with grass; huts of the most common and primitive kind. The church is now taken care of by the Indians, most of whom were off attending a jubilee, or fair, on the other side of the mountain."

Louise Havier and Anita Antone are O'odham basketmakers who frequently stay with Nick and his wife, Birdie Stabel, when demonstrating their traditional crafts to mission visitors. Even though they now live a hundred miles from the mission, they come here because it is a link with their past.

"This church was one of the first ones around that our ancestors could visit," Louise told Nick and me over coffee.

"The first thing they learned from the priests who came from Mexico was about Saint Francis," Anita added. "In some ways we can say that the prayers they learned have been carried on until this day. I was once told that to receive instructions from the priests, four or five women first came all the way from Kaij Mek—you know, Santa Rosa, what we call Burnt Seed Village. But they couldn't be nuns—they had got married—so they just went back to their village and taught the other ones there what they had learned."

Those teachings did bear fruit—most O'odham today still practice what is called "Sonoran folk Catholicism." Some of the Spanish and Italian missionaries also bore fruit when they came to the Santa Cruz—both their own illegitimate progeny and those from imported trees. Padre Juan Bautista Estelric arrived in December 1820 to oversee the placement of over ten thousand adobe bricks being added to the sanctuary and dome of the mission, but rumors of his siring two children forced him to leave by May of 1822. Those who followed him planted five and a half acres of gardens and orchards, including pomegranates, peaches, quinces, and figs. I have personally propagated and transplanted the mission figs of Tumacácori, taking cuttings from an old tree in the courtyard there. Those cuttings have given rise to other cuttings now propagated from Tumacácori clear to Phoenix, moving from one hand to another just as those early O'odham prayers moved from mouth to mouth.

And just as Nick Bleser has kept the stories of Tumacácori moving from mouth to mouth. What he heard from old Manual Contreras, an Opata Indian who tended the mission for twenty years, or from Judy England, the rancher-historian across the street, he passed on to others—Mary Lou Gortarez, Kim Yubeta, and Jim Troutwine, who joined the mission staff after he did. *Oral* histories of our monuments and sanctuaries. They can still loom larger than anything we read in a book or see on a video screen. The wackier the story, the more memorable it will be.

ANGEL HAIRS AMONG THE THREADS

Before I left Tumacácori, I started to hear of other pilgrims who had come just as far as I had already come. One of the workers at Santa Cruz Chile Company told me that her aunt walked from Tucson to Magdalena nearly every year. Anita Antone recalled how ten O'odham women had hiked together from the village of South Komelik the year before, their families providing backup support all the way into Mexico. Like the roadside shrines I had begun to see again, these stories reminded me that I was not alone, but part of a tradition larger and more ancient than any single individual or any single culture.

I had a morning ride through the cottonwood, willow, and elderberry forests between Tumacácori and Nogales. I stopped for a while at Calabazas, a former *visita,* or way station, of Tumacácori's missionaries near the confluence of the Santa Cruz with Sonoita Creek. Calabazas was probably named for the wild relatives of squash that inhabit the Santa Cruz floodplain, one of them being the buffalo gourd, with large, winglike leaves.

Calabazas is still inhabited by two kinds of gourds, but other than that, the scene has shifted considerably since John Bartlett described luxuriant grass and gigantic cottonwoods here in 1852. The sewage ponds of Nogales are in full sight on the floodplain below, as are a half-dozen warehouses for the winter vegetables grown down on the west coast of Mexico. I was beginning to feel the presence of the border nearby—

a higher density of buildings, a thickness in the air from auto exhausts and woodfires for cooking, and more frequent, louder industrial noises all around me. I bicycled one last leg into the twin cities of Nogales, stashed my bike where it would stay for another week or two, and knocked on the door of the home of Susan Spater, a folk historian and friend.

Susan was in there but could not come to the door—she had just had a knee operation a few days before. Her husband, Bill, let me in and directed me to where Susan sat with her knee in a brace, books all around her as if forming a huge nest.

She had invited me to stop by to learn about her work with the binational Pimería Alta Historical Society, but when she saw me limping and I saw her convalescing, we both began to laugh. It looked like a reunion of borderland war veterans.

"Let me tell you about this knee operation," she grinned. "After being disenchanted—even fearful—of modern twentieth-century technology most of my life, I've suddenly had to accept it in the form of surgeons invading my own body. I had gone to several doctors after I tore up the ligaments in my knee, and they all said the same thing: 'Susan, if you don't have surgery, you'll have to cope with limited activity and learn to deal with periodic pain.' So I decided it was time to face what Western science and technology has made possible."

She tossed her hair a little, as if shaking that idea away from her mind, then went on. "At the same time, I've had to accept that I live with the mysteries of Christianity all around me. So many people have been praying for me, on both sides of the border, praying in many different ways. At one point right after the operation, I felt I was being visited by archangels! These archangels with blue wings were hovering in the corners of my room.

"Ohhh, I don't know, I mean, I *was* under the influence of a painkiller drip for my knee at the time, but that doesn't fully explain how I felt." She laughed quietly, as if overcoming the embarrassment of the circumstance. "They were with me, helping me. I'm not saying that the archangels came because of anything I had done. No. It was more like the presence of all those prayers from friends, ones who have a Sonoran Christianity etched deeply into their lives. They did as much for me as the invasion of surgery did, you know? The healing traditions are alive here like nowhere else.

"I guess that's what kept me from being scared. Let me tell you how I went in for this operation. It was five-thirty in the morning, in the sterile halls of Tucson Medical Center. The pre-op interviews and all that paperwork were so cold, I was beginning to panic. I felt isolated, as if even being there was wrong.

"Then, this woman comes in with her scrubs on—I could barely see what she looked like—she had the hair cap and mask on. Then she began to speak to me—in English—but with a lilt, a tone, a pacing that sounded familiar, you know, comforting. I couldn't place it immediately—I had no other clues. So I finally worked up the nerve to talk to her:

" 'Where are you from?'

" 'Well, from here.'

" 'Your name?'

" 'Socorro.'

" 'Socorro . . . what?'

" 'Socorro Murrieta.'

" 'Well, you're from *here,* but where does your family come from?'

" 'From Mexico.'

" 'Where in Mexico?'

" 'Well, a little town in Mexico.'

" 'What part of Mexico?'

" 'Sonora. I come from a little town in Sonora."

" '*¿Cual pueblo Sonorense?*'

" '*Pues, Magdalena de Kino. ¿Porqué?*'

" 'Oh, I am lucky enough to know that place and its saint. And if your roots are there, I can't tell you how glad I am to have you here with me.'

"Socorro's face flashed. And there she was, like my guardian the rest of the operation," Susan sighed, her eyes a little moist.

"The technology couldn't overwhelm that, could it?" I asked.

"No, it couldn't, that's exactly it. Because of the paradoxical kind of spirituality that thrives here. Look at Magdalena's Fiesta where you're headed—paradox. At first, it looks like the spirit of that tradition has been completely overwhelmed, don't you think? The secular, the hedonistic, the commercial, all that stuff. But its spirit is still alive and kicking. That fiesta somehow blends the sacred and secular, the native and the European, the devotional and the celebratory. And because of that, it appeals to Mexicans and Americans alike."

"How long have you been going?" I wondered.

"It was one of the first things I got involved in on my own when I moved here to Nogales to live with Bill. Our Nogales friends later asked me, 'You went there alone, a woman by herself?' It was funny that they asked, for I've *never* feared for my safety or security there amid all those tens of thousands of people from so many walks of life. I still don't.

"In my years with our little Pimería Alta museum, the two exhibits that have been most popular with the community here have been the ones on the Feast of Saint Francis and on the Day of the Dead."

I thought about this for a moment. "The same two feast days are the biggest deals for the O'odham—not even Christmas and Easter seem to be as big in their villages."

"As a historian, I seek out paradoxes—events that cannot be understood from a purely historical framework. If the native peoples of the Sonoran Desert became Roman Catholics as they were instructed, wouldn't Easter and Christmas have become their major holidays?"

I started trying to pull loose ends together before they all went astray: "Well, between the Feast of Saint Francis on October fourth, and the Day of the Dead at the start of the next month—that's harvest time, at least it was for centuries here. It's a time when the people give thanks for the harvest, whatever the earth and little rains have provided.

"Then they leave the dead stubble in their fields while they clean up the *campo santo* for the Day of the Dead. The rains have usually petered out by then, and the fields are left brown—all of a sudden, within one turn of the moon, everything has died. That's when they go out and leave the favorite foods of their deceased loved ones on their graves. Whole families will go. They feed the dead, and I guess the dead feed the living with memories.

"Family time, community time. A communion or thanksgiving. . . . In Sonora, the Day of the Dead has none of that ironic laughing at Death you see in central Mexico. Here, we're just reaching back across the generations and reconnecting everyone to their common sources."

Flying with the archangels.

RISING ABOVE THE BORDER

"Are you going on to the border?" Susan panicked. "It's already getting dark. Aren't you trying to get across to camp somewhere south of town? It's rush hour now, with all that congestion. Are you sure you want to pass through all that for the next ten to fifteen miles before you find a place to sleep?"

Just then, Bill walked into the room. He turned to me. "Look, I have to drive down close to the line to drop something off right now. Why don't you let me take you as close as we can get to the border, and you can walk from there—you'll have a better shot at finding a campsite that way."

Downtown Nogales, Arizona, was jammed with rush hour traffic, and from what I could see of the tangle in Nogales, Sonora, it was even worse. Bill let me out a couple blocks away from the port of entry, with horns honking all around us, with some cars overheating and radiator fluid running out all over the road, while others were double-parked in front of drug and liquor stores, further blocking traffic. Loudspeakers blared out slogans about half-price sales going on, and car radios tried to drown them out with high-volume rock 'n' roll. Instead of walking toward the port of entry, I skirted toward a side street where I could remove myself from the exhaust fumes, the smoke, the steam, and the noise.

Part of me was still back at Susan's, sensing a spirit spanning boundaries, shuttling across a huge loom. Pimería Alta. I had finally arrived at the border, but its presence did not matter to me much—I had been talking with Sonoran mestizos, Chicanos, O'odham, Cora, Euro-Americanos all the way from my point of departure, and no border was so fine a filter that it could sieve out all their sentiments, their legacies into two nicely sorted piles, one for each side of the screen.

I had walked until there was nothing but an eight-foot-high fence in front of me.

Wild buffalo-gourd vines wound up and over it, their wing-shaped leaves cascading down to the other side in Sonora. It looked as if they were rooted on this side, but when I took a good look at where the vines crawled across the ground on the other side of the fence, I realized that they were rooted there as well. That is a peculiarity of the *calabazilla loca*—they rise up from one taproot as the summer rains begin. As they begin to sprawl, every place the nodes of their vines touch moist and fertile earth, they reroot.

I tugged on the vines in a couple places near my feet, and sure enough, they were steadfastly attached to the ground in the margins between the road and the fence. I then reached for the vines rising above me, spilling over the chain-link fence like a wild fountain. They were a little bristly to the touch but felt strong, well anchored, as though they had been growing up out of the ground here, year after year, fence or no fence.

I was in Sonora, the vines behind me, their smell lingering on my hands. I was trying to figure out what to do next, when a man tapped me on the shoulder.

"My name is Pancho. You look like a pilgrim. For the other Pancho, you know, San Francisco, no? I will take you to the edge of the city for half price, four dollars, for I always like to help the *peregrinos* who come here on their way to Magdalena."

I pulled out the little cash I had, and tried to count it in my hands. What he was asking me for was half the change I had left in my pockets. I would still have food and drinks to buy, since I was carrying just two canteens and a small bag of pinole in my knapsack.

"Let me get you off the streets here before it gets dark. South of here, all the way down to the fiesta, you will find families setting up *puestas.* They'll give pilgrims anything they need for along the way. First aid too; they have everything. Once you're south of town here, you'll have no trouble. Several Papago Indians were robbed last year, so why see that happen to you?"

Convinced or conned, I hopped in Pancho's taxi. It was good that I did. Once the traffic began to unjam itself, we passed mile after mile of *maquiladoras,* the assembly plants for products finished with the cheap labor provided by young women who have hardly any other options for work. Most of the workers were gone, leaving only armed security guards. When Pancho finally dropped me off in front of the last junkyard at the south edge of town, it was already pitch-dark.

I was out of the city and back amid the valleys of mesquite and sacaton grass, with Emory oaks straddling the ridges above the road. About fifty miles north of Magdalena, my tender soles told me it was time to hike away from the highway, back into the hills where no one could see my little woodfire for heating tea and tortillas.

I slept curled up in a cloth sleeping bag that night. I dreamed that archangels came, offering me my favorite foods from the desert: mesquite pudding, tepary beans with chiltepines, and saguaro cactus wine. When I finally awoke at four-thirty to a band of coyotes yapping, I felt as if I had been drinking all night.

WHERE STRANDS COALESCE

It was still dark when I stumbled down off the ridge to the side of the highway. Four figures were walking in the same direction not far in front of me. They seemed not to notice my presence, for they were singing and laughing as they walked along.

Sooner or later, I sorted out that it was two young women and two young men, speaking an animated Spanish in the chilly air of the *madrugada*.

As I caught up with them, they asked if I was also on pilgrimage. When I nodded, they offered me breakfast, a seven-ounce can of Bud Light. "We got off work at midnight and left home around three in the morning. If we walk straight on through tomorrow night, we'll arrive in Magdalena the next morning."

"Yeah," moaned one of the women. "Just in time to get back to work in the *maquiladora*."

"Well, at least we are doing our duty for San Francisco," the younger woman said.

"*Sí*," her boyfriend said, turning to me. "*Todos de Nogales adoran San Francisco.*"

By daylight, they were making frequent stops, and after we had passed through the customs checkpoint between Agua Zarca and Cibuta, they told me to go ahead, that they would catch up after a nap. We had dropped down onto a broader, more gravelly floodplain with a scatter of desert willows, wild cotton, and hackberries. Desert broom and cockleburs lined the steeper-sloped channels, while johnsongrass and amaranths stood in thick clusters wherever shallow depressions captured floodwaters for a while. I departed from the highway and walked the meandering channels of the floodplain.

Somewhere after midmorning, I stopped for lunch at Asadero El Molino at the south end of Cibuta village. The lovely young woman at the door looked at me, then went to get her mother from the kitchen. The mother came out, wiping her hands on her apron, and told me that the restaurant didn't usually open for another hour, but because I was a pilgrim, they didn't mind feeding me.

"I'm from Magdalena," the mother offered as she brought me a cup of syrupy coffee, *carne machaca con verduras en chile colorado,* and a dozen thin wheat tortillas the size of large pizzas. "I keep my own *santos* here in the house. I just don't go to fiesta in my hometown anymore. It was prettier in the old days. Now it is all drunks, crooks, hawkers, and hookers. There were more Papagos in the old days, but they're so gentle, everyone has taken advantage of them and they don't come back as much anymore. Even the policemen made money off rolling them, yet the Papagos would never fight back."

As I walked past Rancho Las Bellotas in late morning, I realized that my feet had somewhat recovered from the bruises and blisters of the first couple days, but my toe-nails were lifting off. Sheridan had been right—I was going to lose them. On the other hand, the blisters had just toughened up enough to allow me to move comfortably. Down around my feet, millions of mating grasshoppers made the ground look as though it was jumping. A last gasp to reproduce before drought and cold set in, I guessed—after mating, the females often eat the males, providing them with the stuff they need to ensure that the next bunch of progeny gets on its way.

I was getting dizzy from watching all the conjugations and cannabilisms hopping around at my feet. I climbed a ridge and looked out over the valley. There were giant Mexican blue oaks, orchards of pomegranates and shade-tree dairies, patches of prickly pear plantings, and stacked mesquite-log corrals. Vultures soared above me; kingbirds waged war with each other, sallying out from telephone poles for aerial battles. As I skidded down off the ridge and back through a corn field, I saw that another saint was inhabiting this country: San Isidro, the patron saint of farmers. He walks beside the plowmen like a silent archangel, helping them carry the burden of the plow. His icon was framed and hanging from a tree branch, where a moldboard plow, scythe, and water jug stood in the shade of a hackberry on the edge of the field. With every step I took, it was made clear to me that this was a spirited land, inhabited as much by hardworking saints as it was by hard-loving grasshoppers.

In early afternoon, I moved from one basin to another along a fault line, where earlier upheavals had allowed the Río San Ignacio to flow through a narrow limestone passageway into the broader valley that stretched all the way past Magdalena toward the Sea of Cortés. Here was where I would be dropping back out of oak savanna and mesquite grassland into true desert again. But along those limestone hills, a few artesian springs forced their water up to the surface, creating a small *ciénaga,* or marshland. It had fared far better than the historic *ciénaga* up near San Xaviér.

I dropped down through the hopbush and desert spoons on the limy hill to reach the water of the *ciénaga.* I heard some calling but couldn't see anyone. I took off my shoes and plunged my blistered feet in the water again for the first time since Tubac. The pleasurable chill made the hairs on my neck stand on end.

"We thought you were a desert rat, and yet when we finally find you, you're hovering around water like a spadefoot toad!"

I looked up, and there were two of the truest friends I had: Caroline Wilson and Ginger Harmon. Caroline had driven over from Organ Pipe to meet Ginger in Tucson, and they had gone searching for me, hoping to walk the last leg of the journey. They gave me hugs, then took a good look at me from head to toe.

"Is that suntan or dirt?"

"Oh, my God, look at his feet!"

"What have you done to your body? Look at all those scratches."

"I've been sleeping around with various forms of cactus lately. Sure takes its toll on a man." I was glad to see them.

They helped me into my shoes so that my toenails didn't pop off right there and then. Ginger and Caroline then took turns driving the truck up ahead, so that one of them could walk with me along the way while the other drove or waited.

We walked only a few more miles that afternoon. All around us were pilgrims, little clusters of them. Some hobbled along, alone or in small groups, knowing that they were on the last thirty miles to Magdalena. They had earlier made *mandas*—promises to Pancho—that if he helped heal their sick child, or made them nauseous each time they reached for a whiskey bottle, they would walk for him. Some pilgrims did fifty miles each episode, stringing a journey together over several years. Others did death marches from the mountains of Cananea, the deserts of Gila Bend, the coast of El Golfo de Santa Clara on the Sea of Cortés. Many of them rested in the shade at booths or out on picnic blankets their families had brought, bandaging up their feet, tucking bandannas under their hat brims to keep the sun off their necks. They offered us *horchata,* iced tea, Pepsis, tuna noodle burritos, *tacos de cabeza,* and flat enchiladas. We made quiet, restful conversation with them for a while. When we walked on again, we were happy to be connected, looped into the loom.

Night had arrived by the time we finally reached Imuris, the old O'odham village centered on a cherished image of a black saint. We arranged with a mechanic who lived behind the church to guard the truck the following day while all three of us walked together. We went off and camped on a high mesa above the river valley, where my friends barbecued a delicious meal over a mesquite wood fire. We talked, listened to coyotes howl, and swatted at all the moths and bugs circling in around us for the light of the fire. Too tired to talk any longer, we crawled into our sleeping bags and got what little sleep the bugs would allow us.

WHERE THE WARP MEETS THE WEFTS

The next morning was crisp, clear, and cool. By the time we returned to the pilgrimage route and deposited the truck, we were surrounded by dozens of *peregrinos,* wearing boots, sandals, or walking barefoot; carrying daypacks, walking sticks, and crutches. There were swarms of them. It was the Saturday before the feast, and many of them had been working until evening the night before. Now we formed a river that flowed straight into Magdalena.

Low-riders and balloon-tired luxury pickups cruised up and down the floodplain road, away from the highway, offering support to us in a thousand ways. We were fed egg-and-chorizo burritos, chimichangas, hot coffee, and juice. We were greeted, blessed, and instructed. The floodplain road meandered past old hillside *trinchera* terraces, past stands of organ-pipe cactus and saguaros, past ancient orchards and irrigation canals.

For all the scents and scenes we passed that were strictly Sonoran, there was something undeniably universal about the feel to this last leg of the pilgrimage. It need not have been 1989, in Pimería Alta. It could have been 1840, on the outskirts of Assisi, the Ganges, or Baños, Ecuador. We were drops in a larger historical flow, not solely for Pancho but for any saint, holy man, or virgin who could get us out of our rut. We had broken loose from home to see the land around us and to renew ourselves.

The next village up the road—and the last before Magdalena—was San Ignacio, a place I had been visiting since 1975. When I limped to the door of the Sanchez home, their eyes were filled with friendship and mirth. "So you finally come to see us the right way, on foot! We thought you drove everywhere. [They have had no car most of the time I've known them.] Who are your friends? Come in and have some coffee and fruit!"

The brothers, Jesús and Casimiro Sanchez, grow a dozen kinds of fruit along the floodplain, from quinces and Mexican hawthorns to lemons, apricots, figs, pomegranates, and apple varieties. I have swapped farming advice with them since that first day I stumbled into their tepary bean and chile field more than fourteen years ago. But today, our small talk about crops, weather, and mutual friends was nipped in the bud by their father's presence. Casimiro Senior, born in 1905, couldn't help but comment on the sight of Americans involved in a Catholic pilgrimage. He was widely read and always a freethinker.

"I have lived here most of my life and respect Saint Francis. Still, I cannot bring myself to honor that Padre Kino, the first desert missionary, who is also honored in Magdalena. I'll tell you why," he said wide-eyed, while his daughters politely scurried into the next room to brew more coffee.

"The missionaries, in many ways, were traitors. Traitors to the communities here. Their very presence allowed untold riches to be taken away from here for good. They replaced the ancient gods of mountains, the ancient gods of maize, with these little pictures of European saints. Because we still try to reach these mountains and give thanks for the harvests through these little foreign images, we have become little more than a nation full of paradox!"

"Is he saying what I think he's saying?" Caroline whispered to me, so we asked his permission to pause and translate for Ginger. Ginger nodded in agreement with what she heard. I caught a glance from Jesús, who, being my age, had probably heard his father speak unabashedly like this many times before. He knew it could unsettle strangers, but he also knew that his father's words were not falling on deaf ears.

The old man, lean, unshaven—cowboy hat propped finely on his head—gave us a thumbnail sketch of the history of Mexico, from Cortés, the conquistador, through Miguel Hidalgo y Castillo, the liberator, through the failed promises of Plutarco Elías Calles. Old Casimiro minced no words, testifying to the slavery, corruption, and the wasting of the land's resources which he had witnessed during his lifetime.

"But it's not just Mexican history that tells such a story; it's your history too," he said, leaning over the table toward Ginger and me. "It is a history of devastation that does not only affect us; it has affected the land itself and will do so for many generations."

Casimiro got up and left the room. I was not sure where he was going. He came back with a Mexican newspaper heralding global climate change in its front-page headline.

"You know, it has been hotter and drier here this year than in any year of my life. I *feel* what they are saying in the newspaper—that the temperature is worsening every day. I know that it is not only the ozone layer—is that what they call it?—that is being altered, changing the climate. Think of all the other materials we put into the air—they are drying up the world. Our fields are parched this year. The earth doesn't give of itself anymore. There is simply not enough moisture for the crops, you see? Not enough for the wild vegetation or the wildlife either."

He tipped his cowboy hat back and sighed. "I could show all of this to you by taking you to where I usually harvest the *bledo,* the wild greens I've eaten year after year, throughout my life. This year, the *quelites* arose with the other wild herbs, then burned up before producing anything of value. The sad thing is, it's our own fault, it's what we have put into the atmosphere.

"Well," he added, "this has been a dark story, but you still have the light of the day to walk in. I shouldn't deter you any longer. Come see me again," he said, pressing Ginger's hands warmly into his.

We walked out into the glaring sun of high noon and descended to the shade of the floodplain. The truckloads of families tending the pilgrims had been racing back and forth down the sandy roads for hours now. Their dust hung in the air and in our throats. We stayed mostly silent now, our minds working over what the old man had said, our eyes catching sight of limp, wilted vines on the roadside.

What had begun as a cool, crisp morning was now a hot, hazy day, more like summer than October—the temperature had risen above one hundred degrees again.

And then, before we knew it, we were there, in Magdalena, *en fiesta*. Someone had once said that this rural hub was transformed by fiesta from mouse to rampaging elephant overnight. There were thousands of cars parked or stuck in the streets, swarms of Indians finding their way to their saint, dozens of vendors selling everything from Franciscan robes and medicinal herbs to cotton candy and boom boxes.

We entered the plaza. I saw a Yaqui deer dancer poised for being hunted during the next song, and beside him, a Mexican with a Yankees ball cap selling rubber-band-propelled plastic whirlagigs. In the background, four different loudspeakers roared out announcements, while the drums and horns of a *banda Sinaloense* belched out a march right before us. We wandered over toward the mausoleum that held Padre Kino's bones. It was thick with pilgrims, some on their feet, some on their knees, shuffling through. I was bumped by a short Mayan woman who had her baby on her back wrapped into a blanket. She moved past me, up toward the glass-covered view of the bones of the Jesuit missionary from three centuries before, then showered a handful of copper *ex voto* trinkets down onto the glass—legs, hearts, eyes, ears, arms, and heads. They spilled all over the floor. The Mayan woman crossed herself, then briskly walked out into the open air.

The scatter of body parts lay in front of me. Below them, bones of the first missionary to Pimería Alta who brought the cows and plows, the customs and crops that so quickly shattered what this land had formerly been. He called the land Pimería Alta, but within one hundred fifty years, that cohesive fabric was redesigned, with a political border running across its middle.

I left Ginger and Caroline in the mauseoleum and walked across the plaza one last time to the cathedral. There, in a side chamber, Indians from both sides of the border were lining up for a chance to see their saint. In time, I was allowed to duck into the room, to spend a few moments with a shellacked wooden statue that has come back to life through the touch of hundreds of thousands of hands. I went up to him, touched him on the shoulder, and prayed.

"*Fíjate, San Francisco, ayudenos, por favor,*" I began.

At that moment, I heard an echo, as if others were saying the same all around me. In a half-dozen places around the Sonoran Desert, people had assembled, praying in the same spirit: up in Sells or over in Sure-a-Lot-of-Chickens-Around-Here village on the Tohono O'odham Reservation; across the desert at Jackrabbit-Falls-Down, near Caborca, Sonora; way up in the sierras at the logging town of Maicoba, where the Mountain Pima compete with mestizos for control of the rituals guarding their saint; and far to the north at St. John's Indian School in the outskirts of Phoenix. Outside this cathedral were Yoemem and O'odham, pascola dancers exchanging jokes in honor of him. Dozens of old ladies wailed ancient hymns on his behalf in Sonoyta, Sonora. He seemed to be stretched thin, like an ancient serape, over the entire body of the desert.

"Listen, Pancho," I said, glancing around the room to be sure that no one else was listening to me. "There is more at stake here than the scatter of hands and feet that reach for your help here in this little room. This land needs some healing too. It's gonna take time to reclaim the mined-over hills, to restore the grazed-over range, to reforest the floodplains. Give us the patience to try our hands at that, to reseed the mountains and the clouds. Help us reach our hearts across any borders, any boundaries that have kept us from knowing who and where we are."

A large O'odham lady began to nudge me gently, bumping me, trying to remind me that other people were waiting in a long line to see their saint.

"And Pancho"— I touched his hand again before walking out of the church— "watch out for those lightning storms when they put you up on the roof. A guy could get hurt up there if he doesn't watch out."

Caroline and Ginger were waiting for me as I came out the door. With one of them on each of my arms, I hobbled toward the taxi that would take us back to Imuris, and from there, up through the desert, to the place I call home.

AFTERMATH

I am resting in a small room—in Papago Park on the edge of Phoenix—on the floor, my legs facing a mirror on the door. I look into the mirror to see the bottoms of my feet. It's a terrain I've not often stopped to scrutinize.

What I see is not that pretty to behold. My feet are still bruised and blistered, with corns and callouses on the sides of the small toes. The nails have popped off the big toes on both feet. Blood clots darken the horny tissue exposed where the toenails once were.

Between the toes and the ball of each foot, I see layers upon layers of dead, dried skin flaking away, like the papery outer peelings of an onion. These sloughings of skin must be vestiges of blood blisters. They are stained by the dried puddles of plasma caked between them. The pale, puffy bottoms of my feet look more like storm clouds than like anything I've ever associated with my own body.

I've been rough on them, as rough as men have been on the desert lands I have recently walked through. I close my eyes and move back through the two hundred miles of Arizona and Sonora that I've recently run, biked, backpacked, or hiked. I see scars.

Even within a few hundred yards of my home, I know that there are sorry stories of what has been done to the land. All the cholla ripped clear out of Papago Park to make way for tourists. The local extinction of yuccas. The decline in regeneration of saguaro cactus, as hundreds of jackrabbits do damage to their seedlings in the absence of coyotes. The breeding birds that can no longer find enough grass to cushion their nests inside saguaro boots. They use the plastic tape coming unspooled from discarded casettes instead, nesting in Heavy Metal.

Blistered skin, unhinged toenails. What we do.

One time, Chapo Barnett, the Seri shaman, came up to Phoenix from the Sea of Cortés coast. After several days of demonstrating the making of crafts in museums and shopping malls, Jim Hills, his host, took him, his family, and his friends to Papago Park, thinking that they might want to take a break and walk in a place where there were no escalators.

"I parked our van in the parking lot at the base of the Papago Buttes," Jim explained. "By the time I got out of the vehicle and locked it, the entire gang had taken off for the mountains. Chapo especially—he was running up toward these caves in the rock. I looked up, and it seemed as though Angelita Torres and her sister were jogging up that way too. I start scrambling myself, but by the time I reached Angelita, Chapo was out of sight.

"What in the *hell* is going on? I thought to myself. So I climbed over the top of the ridge—to look down over McDowell Road with all its cars racing by—and there was Chapo, back to a cave, arms spread out, *chanting!* Oh my God! Of course! He had found a place that reminded him of the caves on ridges back along the coast. There in the middle of Phoenix, the Seri had found a place with spirit power: *Aku kama.*"

Spirit power in Papago Park. What we do. What the land does to us.

ABOVE: *Campesino* couple, Guadalupe

OVERLEAF: Bronc rider, Mexican rodeo

Boy with flowers grown by his family for Dia de los Muertos

Evening storm passing south, Tucson

When the Desert Dances the Sonoran Shuffle

Whenever lightning cracked open the darkness hovering over the pueblo, I could catch glimpses of everyone in the streets being doused by a cloudburst. They were sloshing through freshly filled puddles, for this was the first downpour of the summer.

Loads of Sonoran mud turtles rafted down newly formed rapids in places that had been forgotten as riverbeds. Here or there, a displaced desert tortoise could be spotted, trying to find some high ground. Toads had surfaced by the thousands; when a truck careened around a corner into a stream of spadefoots crossing the pavement, it smashed dozens against the asphalt. Young children were running after lumpy Colorado River toads, poking them, singing "*Sapo Verde Soy Yo,*" the nonsensical Spanglish rendition of "Happy Birthday to You."

It *was* a birthday of sorts, a break, a time for starting over. Some desert cultures use the first gully washer of the summer to christen the new year, hoping for better, by God. These thunderstorms have just got to cut the losses suffered over the last few cruel months, for drought, merciless heat, and little verdure have left a heap of bills and carcasses lying around. Little wonder that Sonorans meet these monsoons with a tossing off of shoes, a rolling up of pant legs, and a drinking down of bootleg mescal.

Before, there was a certain tension clogging the air. Now, like a slipknot, it has dis-

I ran into the wet lands confused,
There I heard the Tadpoles singing.
I ran into the wet lands confused,
There I heard the bark-clothed
  tadpoles singing.
In the West the Dragonfly wanders,
Skimming the surfaces of the pools,
Touching with only his tail. He skims
Flapping and rustling wings.
Thence I run as the darkness gathers,
Wearing cactus flowers in my hair.
Thence I run as the darkness gathers
In fluttering darkness to the Singing
  place.
    —Traditional Circling Song of the
      O'odham, in Frank Russell (with
      José Luis Brennan), *The Pima Indians*

Fijate, m'hijito, las aguas han llegado, y por eso, pues, los animalitos estan celebrando con una fiesta.
    —Joaquin Murrieta, *A Field Guide
      to Indigenous Stomp Dances*

appeared. I don't doubt that wildlife can feel this release as much or more than humans can. Over the previous lean months, the animals crowded around the water holes, elbowing one another while trying to steal a decent drink. But *decent* doesn't describe the spoiled, algae-infested soup they found, so thick, it was eaten, not imbibed. Even the best of the kiss-tanks—the longest-lingering pool, shadowed by overhanging rocks—was down to its last come-and-get-me. No wonder a *cimarrón* sheep got run down trying to reach some pathetic excuse for a river nearby—all the *tinajas* were empty. Now that the rains are refilling the potholes and plugged-up arroyos, maybe all those critters won't be breathing down one another's necks.

If a desert storm can bring relief, it can also bring with it a lot of work. The time for idling is gone. Ranchers must make a head-count on their surviving *criollo* cattle— dried beef jerky on the hoof—and move them to where they'll find grass growing and *charco* catchments brimming with floodwaters. Farmers must take to sowing their rain-fed fields with corn, watermelons, and beans before the soil dries out again. Those left without crops and cattle head for the hills and canyons, to work up a lather picking the first flush of wild chiles, a mast of acorns, or a mess of cactus fruits.

After the *campesinos* get a little ahead of their work, they don't at all mind kicking back, to savor the coolness of the evening air. Instead of burning themselves up in the endless work that lies before them—mending fences and repairing roads, weeding fields and driving cattle—some of them make time to dance.

I once stumbled upon such desert dancing at sundown in a dirt-poor Sonoran town, after a hair-raising ride with my *compadre* Tomás. We had just pulled out of a canyon onto hard, wide ground, after driving down muddy watercourses for hours. It had been nerve-wracking four-wheeling, not long behind the flow of one flash flood, not too far in front of another. We had somehow escaped and swore that we would leave such pandemonium behind us for good.

And so, freshly resolved to partake of the passive but watchful life, we pulled up a few chairs at the edge of the cantina's outdoor dance floor and prepared ourselves to survey the sights and sounds of a *norteño* honky-tonk. We idly gazed at the local Tex-Mex *músicos* getting into gear and callously scrutinized all the *señoritas* arriving on the arms of dapper *vaqueros*. Then our eyes gravitated to another sight.

In the middle of the rain-drenched dance floor, about eight feet off the ground, the proprietors had installed a bug zapper: a black-light lure for flying insects, surrounded by electrodes that knocked them dead as they made contact. Each time a moth or fly or beetle was pulled into this bug magnet, it was fried to death by a flash not unlike the lightning still blasting away in the mountains beyond us.

A month or two before, only a few flies would have been electrocuted on a night like this. But with the coming of the rains, the desert had hatched into a tropical carnival. Thousands of metallic green and black beetles appeared, and each one received the shock of its life, dropping dead on the dance floor. Spark after spark added to the heap of invertebrate carnage at our feet.

We became transfixed, half-appalled, half-distraught by this meaty scene. We ordered a round of shots of bootleg mescal, drank, and gawked. The Sonoran cowboys and their high-heeled partners unflappably slogged their way through six inches of carapaces, wings, and antennae. For them, the company of arthropods did not put the skids on their desire to dance. They whirled around the dance floor like dust devils, while the bug zapper buzzed, sparked, and sizzled.

At last, the light show above us and the mescal within us loosened up the celebratory urge. We slugged down the last drops, worms and all. Finding partners to escort us in the promenade, we stepped in with the other couples circling around the black light. Together we danced, stomping bug guts to the tunes of *boleros* and *corridos*. We were brought there, after all, by the same event that had made many bugs bloom, and some of them flash before us: a sudden shifting of seasons, an ordinary world transformed.

Roadside memorial, near Palo Verde Nuclear Plant

Agave murpheyi, descended from plantings made more than five hundred years ago

ABOVE: *Saguaro's grave, Maricopa Mountains*

OVERLEAF: Front-yard shrine to the Virgin of Guadalupe with cactus decorations, Querobabi

Finding the Hidden Garden

Murrieta, California, April 8, 1993: I stared at the hole in the ground in front of me, a hole in the manicured grass. Above it hovered the huge box holding one of my heroes inside it, Howard Scott Gentry. He hated green grass, preferring to sow wild, unruly native plants wherever he lived. It was not only his preference but his trade as well. He was a plant explorer who had spent more than half a century roaming the desert border states, collecting agaves and other wild plants with promise, many of which he brought into cultivation for the first time.

As of April Fool's Day, he was done roaming; this would be the last time he was headed for new ground. His daughters, his wife, his Mexican sidekick Juanito, and many old friends were there to see him off. Some of us served as pallbearers. Others just stood back and cried.

They were ready to lower him into the grave, but I was not ready to let him go. I wished I had one last chance to "talk agave" with him. It would have been too hard to tell him all that he meant to me. Instead, I simply wanted to tell him that I had recently found people still growing, eating, and celebrating the Hohokam century plant, *Agave murpheyi,* a rarity that had posed an unsolved riddle for him for almost thirty years.

I have seen a garden growin' where the rain don't fall.
—Jimmie Dale Gilmore,
"Where Are You Going?"

Un arbol bien plantado mas danzante,
un caminar del rio que se curva,
avanza, retrocede, da un rodeo
y llega siempre.
—Octavio Paz, "Piedra del Sol"

When he and I "talked agave," it seemed that the rest of the world stood still. I could listen to that old man tell me of his plant-exploring adventures for hours. It was odd that we were completely on the same wavelength on that one subject, because whenever we talked about anything else—farming, business, politics, love, marriage, the work of friends, or even the origins of beans—we seldom saw eye to eye. He was forty-nine years my senior, and we had come from different cultures. And yet, we had ended up loving some of the very same things: the smoky taste of home-brewed mescal, the sound of *campesinos* tending maguey, and the diversity of shapes, sizes, and circumstances in which agaves grew.

Once I had invited him down from his home so that he could "talk agave" to a bunch of my friends in a desert garden at night. We sat and drank the fermented, distilled juices of the very plant that was the subject of his rambling lecture. He spoke within the shadow of a giant maguey, and near the end of his talk he glanced over his shoulder at it and declared that, "being a man, I think and speak as a man, but today I also speak for agave. You see me held in the arms of this giant maguey. I am a son of Mayahuel, the goddess of maguey. What I have told you today is what she told me to tell you."

And so old Howard baptized me into some ancient rite, not by water but by firewater—a shot of bootleg *mescal bacanora* distilled from wild desert agaves. Howard became a father figure for me, one whom I sometimes saw as legendary, other times as limited by his own flaws. In turn, I became one of the many grandsons of that Native American goddess, Mayahuel.

I was adopted into Mayahuel's family not long after I left my boyhood home for good, and not too long before my own father died. I had been cooped up on the midwestern farm where I had been working, so I moved to the Sonoran Desert with the hope of devoting my life to tracing the natural history of its plants in the wild. I can now confess I had no idea how I would ever make a living doing such a thing, but I tried. The first regional field guide I purchased after my arrival was a peculiar little book written by Dr. Gentry in 1972: *The Agave Family in Sonora*. I hoped that it would lend me some of the confidence that I sorely needed at the time.

Using it on a long hike down the southern slopes of the Bradshaw Mountains late in the winter of 1975, I easily identified the first two agaves I encountered at higher elevations. I then came on a third that somewhat fit one of Gentry's descriptions but didn't jibe with the distribution map for the same species.

Instead of having flowers on its stalk, it had a bunch of miniature plantlets called bulbils. Judging from what Gentry had written, bulbils seemed to occur regularly only on one species within the Sonoran region, *Agave murpheyi*. However, that species was apparently not known from the lower elevations of the Bradshaws at the time. And so I pressed a specimen, dried it, and sent it off to Gentry a few weeks later. I had learned in the meantime that he had "retired" to Arizona, leaving the U.S. Department of Agriculture as its chief plant explorer to take on the somewhat honorary position as senior research scientist at the Desert Botanical Garden.

Within a week of sending off the specimen, I received a letter from Gentry on some self-designed stationery embellished with a sketch of a flowering maguey: "Welcome to the Agave Family!" he proclaimed.

His letter went on to inform me that if a certain kind of agave is damaged by freezes as it begins to flower, it will abort its blossoms and reproduce vegetatively, spawning through bulbils like the ones I saw. "I don't think it would be much fun if we could replicate ourselves that way," he added dryly. In short, the identity of my plant was not definite: it could be *Agave murpheyi*, or a related species that didn't normally produce bulbils. Gentry encouraged me to make more collections at the same site. In that way, we could verify whether or not bulbils were characteristic of the entire population. He also invited me to pay him a visit sometime. I did.

Within a year of that first dispatch from the old man, I embarked on my own agave-collecting trips in Sonora and tasted bootleg mescal for the first time. My father had died while I was out of reach, in Mexico. After the funeral I took my dried plants to Gentry, to see if the master would help me interpret their value. We soon found something to talk about on a fairly regular basis. Within another year, I took a few weeks off to work with him. We began by drinking tequila in an agave patch on a Fourth of July evening and stayed together until the end of the summer, when I left for more plant collecting. We split our time between two places, the Desert Botanical Garden in Phoenix and his family's homestead in Murrieta, nestled within the Sierra foothills an hour south of Los Angeles.

That summer, ethnobotany and the horticulture of native plants became more than technical sciences for me; they harbored a reservoir of stories about rural peoples and their ties with the natural world. Nearly everywhere in the American deserts, agave fibers formed the rope that secured those ties. Gentry considered this link a "mutualism between two disparate organisms"—a true symbiosis—for without agaves as his companions in the desert, "man would be a lone egocentric without a single other organism in the whole world to counsel him."

The old man would draw upon the counsel of mescal or scotch each afternoon before wandering off to his bedroom for a siesta, or falling asleep, glass still in hand, in his easy chair on the patio. He always kept a good field hat on while he was outside and often kept a little wild stubble on his chin to go along with it. Lubricated by his afternoon drink, he might recall the views of scholars (Webb, Sauer, or Xolocotzi) on some arcane horticultural practice of Mexican Indians. Then he might give me an Indian perspective on the same practice, by referring to a conversation he had with a Guarijio, Mayo, or Tarahumara elder forty years before. If I was lucky, he might recall one of his own adventures while out exploring the sierras with Juanito Arguelles, who had often traveled with Gentry as his *mozo,* or errand boy. Arguelles has ended up being the second most prolific collector of agaves in the history of northern Mexico, but the collections with his name on them hardly rival the twenty-five thousand or so that bear Gentry's name. A fourteen-year-old when Gentry first met him in San Bernardo, Sonora, in 1933, Juanito learned to take care of Gentry's mules and plant presses. He later moved to Murrieta and found jobs tending cutting horses; he decided to retire years before his former boss had to force himself to stop working.

Once Gentry began his stories from the trail, they would unwind naturally. He often returned to a point he had wanted to demonstrate to me earlier in the day. When recording folk taxonomies for plants, he insisted, be careful of *campesinos* making up provisional names for plants in areas unfamiliar to them. Then he would laugh heartily and confess that in 1951, he had provisionally named one species *Agave jaiboli* after what he thought was an Indian name. In the Sierra de la Ventana, he had encountered a *gente de razon* (non-Indian) who told him that a fine distilled drink could be made from this unusually sweet plant. The man had called the distilled drink *jaiboli,* to distinguish it from the mescal that the Guarijio Indians made from *temeshi,* another local agave.

Fourteen years later, Gentry ran into the man again and learned that he had worked as a wetback years before on the U.S. side of the border. While in the United States, the man had taken a liking to the highballs that the Gringos made with their liquor. "*Aquí, hacemos jaibolis con mescal,*" he told Gentry, who belatedly realized that *jai-*

boli was no Indian word after all. The name stuck nonetheless, and Gentry used it for the official scientific name when describing the plant as a new species in 1972.

While we were over in California, Gentry took me for my first drive through the heart of Los Angeles. We were on our way to the Huntington Botanical Gardens, one of the most heavily visited horticultural displays on the West Coast. There in the middle of its outdoor exhibit, the old man pulled out a rope and made it into a lasso. He deftly tossed the loop over a twenty-foot-high agave stalk in flower and fruit. Once he caught its candelabralike bouquet, we wrestled it down to the ground, much to the horror of the tourists passing by.

"I've been waiting for this plant to flower damn near since the year you were born," he said, taking his hat off and wiping the sweat from his brow on his shirtsleeve. Gentry had planted dozens of seedlings of unknown species at Huntington in 1951 and 1952, but it took some of them another quarter century to flower for the first time. It was only then that he could fully describe them.

"Take my machete," he ordered, "and cut three or four of those leaves off. Skin 'em out and section them so that they fit into the plant press. I'll finish up pickling the flowers while you're doing that." The entire effort took nearly two hours and filled an entire plant press. Every day the following week, I swabbed each leaf section with alcohol to keep it from molding and dried the blotters out in the sun. After waiting twenty-five years to finish his work on this collection, Gentry was not about to let a specimen go to waste.

Hundreds of such specimens informed his 670-page masterwork, *Agaves of Continental North America,* which was finally published in 1982 nearly fifty years after Gentry had begun his first agave collections. By that time, the old man seemed tired and frustrated by what he had done. "It only makes evident how little I know," he said sadly. "But I just can't do any more. These damn plants have nearly killed me. It's up to you young lads and lassies now."

Even before he reached this stage of exhaustion, he had encouraged me to ask O'odham friends questions he himself had not resolved. He was especially curious about their knowledge of *Agave murpheyi,* because its distribution puzzled him. He'd seen it just north of Phoenix, then not again until one hundred miles south in an O'odham Indian village, and then not for another hundred fifty miles southwest in Sonora, near another O'odham village. His masterwork contained just three cryptic lines about its origin and distribution: ". . . *murpheyi* has never been observed in extensive or dense populations. Some of the clones appear to have been associated with old Indian living sites. The propagules are easily transported and transplanted."

The plant happened to grow in the garden of Laura Kerman, the namesake and godmother of my daughter. Laura was an O'odham potter, teacher, and storyteller who was older than Gentry but just as horticulturally curious. When I asked her about the origins of her plants, she nodded toward the Baboquivari Mountains.

"When I was a little girl, we would stay with my grandmother back in those mountains during the dry season. We took these plants from there. There used to be hundreds of them up in the canyons, and that is what my people would harvest to eat. They would dig them up, chop off the long leaves, roast them in a pit overnight."

Her eyes would get wide as she began to visualize scenes from her childhood. "Next day, they opened the pit to take them out. If the coals were still warm, they took the leaves they had cut earlier and dried them over the coals. Then they would make rope or other weavings out of the fibers taken from the leaves. We never made mescal to drink, like the Mexicans do, although some of the old men would buy it from the Mexicans and then get drunk. We just ate it and used it to make rope."

Then she looked up at me, blinking. "You take me up to the mountains for a picnic, and I'll show you those plants."

One summer, I did take Laura up to the canyon home of her grandmother. We had a picnic with a small band of Pima, Papago, and Navajo friends, then she sent us up the slopes looking for plants. But as we scrambled around the abandoned village, we could find only the more common species of desert agave, no *murpheyi*.

I was sure that she had not confused the two. She simply called the common desert agave *a'ud* but knew the one in her yard as *a'ud nonhakam*, "the agave that has eggs or progeny." In fifteen years of hiking the Baboquivaris, I had found only a single *murpheyi*-like plant that had "progeny" or bulbils on its stalk where flowers might otherwise be. As with the first agave I ever collected, I could not be sure of its identity by this one trait alone. Its leaves were too dried to allow for identification. My only guess is that Laura's ancestors had cultivated this special agave around their homes in the last century, but it had not survived the droughts, freezes, cows, or harvesters. Its fiber and food qualities were so superior to those of *Agave deserti* that younger O'odham harvesters may have finished off (or transplanted to their own homes) the plants their forefathers had tended.

I later decided to return to the only area in Sonora where Gentry had seen *murpheyi* growing. It was an area that I knew had old, mostly abandoned O'odham villages and ancient hillside terraces nearby. Gentry had found *murpheyi* cultivated in a yard across from a truck stop, but its owner claimed that it came from the nearby hills where it grew wild. And yet, when Gentry got up to go and explore the hills, the Sonoran dissuaded him, saying that the plants there had already been cut for eating and for making bootleg mescal.

It seemed easy enough to travel forty miles south of the border and explore the hills surrounding San Luisito to find what might be a truly wild population of the plant. But, like Gentry, I would not see any plants in the hills. As my friends and I drove into San Luisito one summer day, a roadblock loomed up just fifty yards past the garden where the plants grew. Since we weren't going any farther south, I pulled into the truck stop rather than driving right up to the Federales and their barriers. Unfortunately they thought I was dodging them.

The next thing I knew, five Uzi machine guns were pointed at me, and two other armed guards had me up against the hood, frisking the daylights out of me. Two hours later, after my Jeep Cherokee had been scoured for every smidgeon of plant debris, and each leaf analyzed for traces of drugs, the narcotics squad released me and my friends.

"This is drug country, why did you come down here anyway?" the *jefe* asked me. I pulled out Gentry's *Agave Family in Sonora* and showed him a picture taken in the garden across the road some twenty years before. He was not impressed. He doubted that I had any legitimate reason to be there and discouraged us from wandering around in the hills nearby. "There are drug traffickers who think they can go around us. They are not the kind of people who will like you getting in their way."

The following winter, after I had heard that drug running through that part of Sonora had waned, I did find four or five more ranchos with little patches of *a'ud non-hakam* in their yards. Always, the O'odham and mestizo cowboys would tell me the same thing they told Gentry. Years ago, they had brought these plants in from ones in the hills, but now they were no longer sure if there were any left in the wild.

About that time, however, word came in from a friend in New River, Arizona, that caught me off guard. I had begun to work at the Desert Botanical Garden, joining Gentry's department. Another one of Gentry's understudies, Wendy Hodgson, had been collaborating with an amateur botanist, Rick DeLamater, tracking the distributions of agaves in central Arizona. One day Rick heard me complain to Wendy about my trouble finding truly *wild* populations of *Agave murpheyi* anywhere on the O'odham Reservation or in Sonora.

"Crap, I know where a bunch of wild *murphs* are right by my home. You know Encima de la Mesa near New River?" Rick said casually.

"There are prehistoric terraces all over there!" I blurted.

Rick didn't follow me. "What do terraces have to do with it?"

"There's this archaeologist named George Gumerman who had a big project up there in the seventies, and I went up there with him one time. He had a whole team of students mapping hundreds of terraces and rock alignments built prehistorically, thinking that they might have been used for agriculture. Funny thing was, in all their excavations and analyses of pollen and soil, they never figured out what people could have been growing up there. You haven't seen any prehistoric agricultural features where the agaves are?"

Rick looked at Wendy and scratched his beard. "All I know is where the plants are. And where a few hilltop ruins are above them. I wouldn't know a prehistoric agriculture feature if it reared up and bit me on the . . ."

By the end of the week, Wendy, Rick, and I went up to New River with some biologists visiting from Mexico and the Navajo Reservation. As we walked out across the *bajada* toward the plants, I began to see rock pile after rock pile, rock alignments, check dams, terraces, and stone tools. Rick led us to one particularly large clone of agaves. There in the middle of it was a prehistoric agave knife, the same kind that had been found near agave roasting pits throughout the Southwest for decades. And there, beneath the *a'ud nonhakam,* was the lip of a cobblestone border that had been put there to slow the flow of water down the slope at least five or six centuries before.

The hidden garden. There, amid the paloverde and mesquite, the bur sage and the barrel cacti, a prehistoric Hohokam crop had persisted at least half a millennium after being last tended. The same plant—the identical genetic stock that had been transplanted here in prehistoric times—had reproduced vegetatively on its own, clinging to the same terrace where it had been originally placed. Rick had discovered the hidden garden, a horticultural experiment so well adapted to the desert that it ultimately needed no human intervention to keep it going.

By that time, we knew that tens of thousands of acres of similar rock-pile fields, cobblestone alignments, and terraces had been found between Tucson and Phoenix by Paul and Suzanne Fish. At first, they too were baffled because Suzanne's pollen analysis revealed no obvious candidate for the crop that the Hohokam had grown there.

Then one day, Paul's survey team stopped to eat lunch on the *bajada* slope. Nudging his bootheel into the slope overlooking a wash, one of them noticed that they were sitting on ash and charcoal, not soil. The team had stumbled upon a huge roasting pit, and within a few weeks their coworker Charlie Miksicek had sorted out fragments of agave leaves mixed into the ash. The leaves were too beat-up to identify, but when Charlie heard of Rick finding *Agave murpheyi* up at New River, it didn't surprise him. Most of the agaves would have been cut and roasted before they flowered anyway. If *murpheyi* aborted its flowers so early, it's no wonder that Suzanne could find little pollen where Charlie had found an abundance of charred leaves.

Suzanne, Paul, and Charlie gradually fleshed out the details of a prehistoric horticultural tradition in North America. It was a tradition that had escaped the notice of dozens of archaeologists who had worked in the same region over the last century.

They had presumed that agaves were aboriginally cultivated nowhere north of Mesoamerica. Paul and Suzanne Fish have now shown otherwise, that agaves have been intentionally cultivated in Arizona since A.D. 600. The one hundred fifty square miles of rock piles on the middle *bajada* above Marana captured and conserved water for each vegetative transplant, augmenting food production in an area too high and dry for conventional irrigation agriculture.

The agaves grown from Marana to New River were not simply transplanted wild species but specially selected variants. They had all the characteristics of other domesticated plants such as the maize and thornless prickly pear brought in from Mesoamerica. The Hohokam leaders living down near the better-watered ceremonial centers had likely grubstaked workers to cultivate agaves, offering them maize and beans grown on rich floodplain soils in exchange for mescal and fiber. Thus, the scenario that Gentry had earlier imagined for prehistoric agave cultivation in Mesoamerica rang true for arid America as well:

> They cleared wild land and put agave into it. They opened up new niches for the random variants of the gene-rich agave.... They selected the genetic deviants of high production by planting vegetative offsets. Generally, this is what man did for agave in this Mesoamerican symbiosis.
>
> In return agave has nurtured man. During the several thousand years that man and agave have lived together, agave has been a renewable resource for food, drink, and artifact.... As man settled into communities ... agave fostered the settled habit, attention to cultivation, and the steadfast purpose through years and life spans, all virtues required by civilization.... Agave civilized man.

It is even more amazing that the agaves did not become civilized. The *a'ud non-hakam* had never lost its capacity to survive, to thrive in desert climes without the aid of irrigation or gardeners.

Over the following years, Rick DeLamater and Wendy Hodgson found remnants of more than fifty previously neglected stands of *Agave murpheyi* in the forests, parks, and ranchlands of central Arizona. Rick's eye for this plant became legendary. Every once in a while, he would come into our office, sure that he had found a truly wild population. On further inspection, Rick, Wendy, or I would find artifacts, rock alignments, and other cultural remains to indicate prehistoric cultivation. I found another five sites in Sonora on my own, but all of them were associated with historic homesteads and prehistoric settlements. They could persist amid wild vegetation but were never found in "pristine wilderness"—their presence always spoke of earlier cultural presences, of man-made desert gardens from long ago.

Even their genetic history showed human imprints. We sent leaf samples to geneticist James Hickey, who discovered that all the plants had the same chemical markers regardless of whether they came from Sonora, Papaguería, or New River—they had none of the heterogeneity from site to site found in wild agaves. Perhaps they were all of one clone, transported and then transplanted over hundreds of square miles in the heart of the Sonoran Desert. And yet, they all took that desert to heart, adapting to its droughts and freezes, resisting its pests and plagues in a way that few of today's pampered crops could if cut loose from human attention. The hidden garden could get along with or without the intervening hand of Hohokam horticulturalists.

In the end, that is what Dr. Gentry let us do. He never intervened with our agave studies, all of them ultimately grounded in his own. He never expressed any worry over whether younger investigators would come along to revise parts of the story that he had spent most of his life compiling. He encouraged Mexicans as well as North Americans to get out into the field and prove him right, wrong, or somewhere in between. After he retired, he would still listen to our new reports as they came in, but he would never try to give these new details his own spin. He would shift uneasily between his respirator and his afternoon drink, then mutter in his throaty voice, "Pshaw, laddie, you've come up with something there that I would have never expected!"

The last couple years of his life, I saw the old man less than I had seen him over the previous fifteen years. He could no longer get out into the field with any frequency, and I guessed that confinement killed his spirit. I could not stand to see him captive in a domestic scene—a field man relegated to the subtle insults of idle retirement, nursing homes, or hospitals. Instead, I took the memory of him into the field with me, trying to seek out the kind of *campesinos* with whom he had loved to talk since he first crossed into Mexico sixty years before.

Francisco Gamez Valenzuela was one such man, the kind of Sonoran that Gentry have would fallen in with—two kindred spirits. I rounded a corner in Querobabi, Sonora, one summer day, and there was this yard, spilling over with all kinds of desert plants, including a long hedgerow of *Agave murpheyi*. I stopped my van in the middle of the road and looked around to see if anyone was hidden within all that verdure, working in the yard. And there was Francisco, who was more than willing to talk about the plants he called his *lechuguilla*.

"*Hace diez años que se tranplantó aquí. Se crece en las lomas de piedra cerca de Ranchos San Jacinto, El Saucito, La Sesma . . . ,*" he told me, rattling off the names of abandoned historic outposts from which he had salvaged these plants a decade ago. I asked him if they were truly wild, or whether they appear to have been associated with the former plantings of his *antepasados.*

"Pues, se crece silvestre, pero hay corrales de piedras, trincheras, y rastras de minería en aquellos cerros." With cobblestone corrals, terraces, and remnants of rustic mining operations, the sites could have been from the colonial period, if not earlier.

Francisco told me how he occasionally roasted a single plant into the smoky, caramelized foodstuff called *mescal tatemada.* He also loved to join forces with an elderly neighbor now and then to pit-roast twenty to forty "pineapples," then distill them into *mescal lechuguilla.* I took a look at his hedgerow. It was obvious that he took good care of the plants—they were a deep blue-green and stood waist high.

I asked him if they needed much pampering. The answer he gave me made me realize that *Agave murpheyi* would still do fine long after Howard, Francisco, and I were all long gone. I thought about it long after translating it in my head: "Oddly enough, it produces much better during the drought than it does during wet years," he said, tipping his cowboy hat back on his head.

"What?" I'd never heard of such a thing for a domesticated plant.

"Pues, sí, durante la sequia, se da mas ley." During the hardest of times, a Sonoran folk-saying goes, a good plant still "gives the law." The Law of the Desert. Not only had *Agave murpheyi* persisted as part of local diet and drink, it also remained strongly rooted in the folk expressions of the village.

When I returned to visit Francisco the following December, I was just in time to catch the Hohokam agave resurrected in a new spiritual role. As I entered Querobabi, I began to notice shrines erected for the Virgin of Guadalupe, who was honored during a series of processions culminating on her feast day of December twelfth. The families in Querobabi had each constructed what looked like miniature desert gardens in front their homes, replicas of the hill of Tepeyac, where the Virgin communicated with the Mexican Indian Juan Diego in December of 1521. There on the little hills erected around the village, *Agave murpheyi* rosettes stood alongside pictures and statues of the Virgin.

According to legend, Juan Diego had converted to Catholicism from his native religion but still felt that this was not the path for all his people. As he climbed a hill one day, the Virgin appeared in order to assure him that she would remain within his indigenous community. He went down into the Valley of Mexico and spoke of his vision to Bishop Zumarraga, who refused to believe that the Mother of Christ would offer anything of import to a lowly Indian.

Juan Diego prayed to the Virgin to receive some sign that he could take to Zumarraga, to convince the bishop of the veracity of his claim. That is when the Virgin appeared again, urging Juan Diego to climb to the very top of the Loma de Tepeyac to pick flowers for the bishop. Juan Diego hesitated, knowing that few flowers grew on the arid, rain-shadow slopes of the valley in winter. Nevertheless, he decided to follow her instructions.

By all accounts, he found Roses of Castille "growing in a place where Nature produces only cactus and maguey." He wrapped these domestic roses of European civilization in his cloak, and when he offered them to the bishop, he found the miraculous image of the Virgin imprinted on the inside of his serape. This began the veneration of the Virgin of Guadalupe as the matron of Mexican Indians, a tradition that became strongly rooted as far north as Sonora by 1740.

In the Sonoran folk tradition, cacti and agaves from the local desert are transplanted into shrines for the Virgin to commemorate the arid landscape where she first made contact with their people. Organ pipe, fishhook, and pincushion cacti are nestled side by side with the *lechugilla* offshoots taken from Francisco's hedgerow, and visited by the processions for the week prior to the Virgin's feast. Then, crepe paper flowers of the Castillian Rose are added to the shrines, while the matron of all indigenous people sees her miracle observed once again.

From the embrace of the goddess of Mayahuel to that of La Virgin de Guadalupe, this native plant had somehow survived the collapse of the Hohokam ceremonial life to be resurrected and integrated into the folk Catholicism of Sonora.

From deep in my memory, I heard Gentry's prophetic words:

> As civilization and religion increased, the nurturing agave became a symbol, until with its stimulating juice man made a god of it. . . . Mayahuel, the principal goddess of agave, slaked the parched throat, relieved the duty pressures, altered the spirit, provided at least temporary surcease from hard life, and, being god-like, protected the home. Altogether, this was another contribution of agave to man during the centuries of the symbiosis.

It seemed the agaves joined with the Virgin in desert gardens to produce many of the same effects. Mayahuel now stood in the background, but her work, too, was being carried on.

In April 1993 Mayahuel witnessed one of her sons rejoin the earth—one who felt more comfortable on the cactus-and-maguey-stippled slopes of Mexico than in the suburbs of the United States. He was being buried in one of those suburbs, and neither Mayahuel nor the Virgin were being mentioned in the funeral service. I stood in the back row, listening to the cadence of the ceremony, scanning the surroundings. The memorial service was not all that different from those offered for other well-respected elderly men in Protestant enclaves within southern California. As the minister closed his hymnal, and the audience began to stir, I felt crestfallen, as though something were desperately missing.

Marie Gentry, his widow, must have sensed that same feeling, because she stopped us all dead in our tracks right as the service ended.

"Thank you, all of you, for being here with us for this service. But because it has all been offered in English, someone who is here was not able to share in the eulogies. It is someone who spent nearly as much time as I spent with Howard in those early days, and because Spanish is his native tongue, I would like to ask Juan Arguelles to say something in Spanish before we all go. Juanito, *por favor . . .*"

There were a few Spanish speakers among us, but this request caught most of the crowd off guard—they shifted uneasily in their Sunday clothes as Juan moved forward through the crowd. He came to the hole in the earth and spoke to it, as if beginning a slow but steady mouth-to-mouth resuscitation.

"Pues, este viejito—es uno de mis grandes amigos. Con este señor, he caminado a todos partes de la sierra, buscando para plantas . . ."

And with that first step, Dr. Gentry's sidekick began to conjure up the trails they had traveled together, on horse, on foot, in Model T; he told of the amazing plants they had discovered, the mescal they had sampled; he called up the campfires they had hovered around and the stories they had heard there—stories that had never been written down, but had been passed from mouth to mouth, campfire to campfire, for centuries, and still no doubt lived on wherever Mayos, Guarijios, Tarahumaras, and others came together around a mescal pit in the dry sierras.

And that was when I remembered that ethnobotany is not just a science. It's a reservoir of stories that link humankind with the verdant earth, a reservoir of legends we need to dip into now and again. The stories are not restricted to indigenous peoples. They honor the spirited plants they relied on for food, for drink, for miracle. Because we all owe the land and its plants our lives, such stories speak for all of us. They must reach from the past into the present, to hook farmers and ranchers and even suburban gardeners, linking them to what nourishes and inspires us. The best remind us of that capacity for symbiosis, a capacity one old crusty ethnobotanist found in the legend of Mayahuel. If we leave behind that capacity to be part of mutualisms larger than ourselves, then the rest homes, suburbs, and plant engineering labs will turn darker and lonelier, more sterile than ever before.

Woman with house made of adobe and saguaro ribs

Casa Grande ruins with protective rain shelter

Chico Suni and his house of found materials on land long inhabited by his family

Re-storying the Sonorous Land

EXTINGUISHING THE SOUND OF SUMMER HEAT

Out of nowhere, it seemed, the deafening noise of airplane engines turned up. It overwhelmed everything: the rasp of cactus wrens, the drone of cicadas, and the tales being shared between Seri Indians who sat together in the sand. The blaring motors forced all of them to stop their stories and songs. They glanced up from the beach edging the Sea of Cortés and saw an airplane landing. On that June day in 1993, the "sound of summer heat"—a humming the Seri had heard in their homeland for centuries—was supplanted by another, more commonplace noise.

While the engines still roared, the governor of the State of Sonora deboarded the aircraft and shook hands with Seri leaders. He then announced what everybody already knew: the Solidarity Program had at last brought electricity to this, the only tribe of traditional hunters-gatherers remaining in the entire Mexican republic.

With a cut of a ribbon and a flick of a switch, lights, televisions, and *licuadora* blenders all spun into action. The governor quickly waved good-bye, reboarded, and left. The noise of motors swallowed up the crashing of the waves, the crying of the animals, the very sound of desert summer itself.

For the land the time has come
The sound of summer heat passes through
  the desert
The sound of summer heat pervades the
  desert . . .
The summer heat's sound has spirit power.
                    —Juan Mata, Seri shaman

That desert—its firmness, resilience, and fierceness, its whispered chants and tempestuous dance . . . shaped us as geography always shapes its inhabitants. The desert persists in me, both inspiring and compelling me to sing about her and her people, their roots and blooms and thorns.
—Pat Mora, "The Border: A Glare of Truth"

That's when the bartering began. Two handwoven baskets for one satellite dish, one wooden figurine of a dolphin for a floor fan. Within weeks, the Seri were swapping limberbush baskets, ironwood carvings, miniature balsa rafts, beads, dolls, and bull-roarers for dozens of electric radios, swamp coolers, televisions, videocassette recorders, and more satellite dishes.

Alfonso Torres laughed as he told us how he traded two *sapeem* baskets made by women in his family for the first *parabolica* dish to be set up in the village. (Weeks later, when I mounted a plastic Frisbee atop our temporary ocotillo-frame hut in the middle of the village, the Seri kids doubled over, squealing with laughter, "See, the Gringos have a *parabolica* for their home too!")

"It was easy," Alfonso grinned, "some Americans we had known for a while brought us the dish and even set it up. The women had been working on these baskets for a couple months, knowing that we might get the *parabolica* in exchange for them. Since then, these women spend their time making baskets while watching the *foto-novela* soap operas. The boys love the *box* and the *futbol*. You know, we get programs from Mexico City, Hermosillo, Los Angeles, everywhere."

Then he smirked. "We have just learned that the people from Los Angeles can take their clothes off on TV after midnight. What do you call it, *la porno-graphía?* . . . Unfortunately, we have so many people who must sleep in the room where we keep the television that it is hard to have it on after midnight. I have seen the Americans without clothes only once, when the rest of the family was away seeing relatives in Desemboque."

One night, after the shows from Los Angeles had been turned off in the surrounding households, I listened for the other sounds that have filled the air at Punta Chueca for centuries. The sound of kindling being snapped and stoked into a campfire. Dogs barking at shadows passing over them. The *ai'inamoka,* a wind that blows from land to sea. The surf crashing on the cobble beach north of us, louder than that on the sandy beach closer to our hut.

I heard Chapo, the fifty-eight-year-old shaman, shaking a rattle and singing a whale song in a low voice. I heard Miguel Barnet tell of dreams he had in 1941 of a singing cave, ones in which a very hot wind howls through a door, dreams that he drew pictures of with the very first crayons he had ever held. I heard a child crying out in his sleep, followed by the comforting pats and coos of his mother as he fell back to sleep.

I heard all of this, interrupted by one last radio playing "I can't get no satisfaction," or a heavy metal cover of it in Spanish translation.

It was already late at night when Ernesto Molino wandered into our camp. He was eager to hear what we had learned about the war going on amid the Mayan Indians of Chiapas, a war between the Mexican army and the Zapatista guerrillas. He recalled the times in Seri history when his forefathers skirmished with the same Mexican army, in the 1850s, 1890s, in 1904, and finally, in the 1920s.

His grandfather had told him details of these battles, details that haunt him to this day: of the time when Seri men had left camp to scare up some food, leaving the women behind in a cave on Isla Tiburón. While the men were gone, the army found where the women and children were hiding. The troops shot all of them down, then heaped up the bodies in four huge piles. When the Seri men returned, the soldiers were gone. There amid the piles, one child was alive, crying, trying to suckle his mother's breast. Ernesto gulped. "When the child saw his father, he asked why his mother wouldn't wake up, to talk to him and to feed him."

Ernesto carries hundreds of such stories around in his head. "I don't have a television, don't need one," he said. Still, he pointed to all the antennae on the houses around him and shrugged; their noise now seemed inescapable. I asked him if he still hears enough of the older, more familiar sounds at night. He shook his head sadly, saying that he fears the changes that the television itself is bringing, but he fears waking up to another sound as well: "I worry that one day I will wake up to the sound of machine guns here, as they are hearing today in Chiapas."

RECAPTURING THE SONGS

The next morning, a Gila woodpecker woke me up. It was drilling at the metal fan turret atop one of the Seri's concrete block houses. The wind flapped the tarps covering our ocotillo hut. I crawled out of my sleeping bag, snapped up the buttons of my pants and shirt, pulled on my boots, and wandered out beyond the village edge. I turned inland, and after a few minutes, I found myself deep in a towering cactus forest of cardon, saguaro, and organ pipe. It was there that I stopped to listen to the sounds that have been here as long as this place has been desert.

It was early enough that Bendire's thrashers were still moving from shrub to shrub, repeating a *chuck, chuck, chuck* before letting loose with a melodic warble. They stayed low, as did the gnatcatchers, who buzzed along as they went, flicking their tails up and down. Coveys of Gambel's quail scurried through the washes, mulling and grunting along until one of them got scared. Then they all broke into flight, wingbeats booming.

The cactus wrens would stop rasping whenever they heard such a racket. And the mockingbirds would stop imitating the cactus wrens, dropping down from their perches and staying silent until all signs of danger had passed. Gila woodpeckers glided away from me, annoyed, settling on a giant cardon a hundred yards away. More gnat-catchers followed them, moving in the same direction.

The high white butts of antelope jackrabbits crashed through the burrobushes and elephant trees as they ran for deeper, darker cover. And atop every large tree, phainopeplas *whurp*ed and fluttered. Flycatchers sallied out, *prrt*ing, then sallying back again. Towhees flitted through, *peek*ing from behind every branch. Such notes announce the Sonoran Desert to my ears, the same way the giant saguaro cactus defines it for my eyes. Sonorous melodies. Like the volatile smell of creosote bush, they tell me that I have come home, home to a chorus of trilling birds, rattlers, cicadas, and coyotes. My family. The desert family choir.

Farther off in the distance, I heard ravens and grackles cackle and whistle while they scavenged along the beach. They lured me to the water's edge, where I heard ospreys and long-billed curlews taking flight and caught the splash of a flock of Mexican wood ducks rising up out of the surf. I was not *anywhere* in the desert. I was in a peculiar spot unlike all others, where an extra-salty sea washes up onto the driest of sands. Maps call this stretch of water between Sonora and Isla Tiburón the Canal de Infiernillo. I suspect it would have made a much better name for an all-night TV station broadcasting out of Los Angeles, because what it means is the "channel of hell."

FINDING THE DRONE WITHIN US

A couple of years ago, I had to go halfway around the world, to another desert, to learn that natural and manmade music can form a tenuous harmony. My wife, Caroline, and I spent a blustery night with two Aussie mates in the Red Center of their continent. Marlene and Dennis Chinner drove us out in their Fore-Runner from Alice Springs into the gravelly bed of the Hugh River. We heaped up branches of river red gums to make a huge bonfire, then sat in our swags, drinking and listening to the sound of the desert riparian forest reverberating in the night.

It was a deep bassy drone, one you felt in your chest, as if your body cavity had become an amplifier for some insect chant. There were thousands of cicadas there, to be sure, but something else—something larger, more ancient—thrummed in the dark. It was the desert forest, resonating, like the heartbeat of the entire, fire-charged arid continent.

Two nights later, during a native-foods feast of "bush tuckers" baked in the coals of a second gumwood campfire, another friend brought out his didgeridoo, a six-foot-long wind instrument, made from the trunks of trees hollowed out by termites in Arnhem Land. I've heard the aboriginal word *didjeridu* imitates the circular pattern of tongue movements that musicians use when playing the instrument, as they shape the wind they blow into the trunk. It comes out the other end of the trunk sounding like, well, the forest itself: deep, haunting syllables reverberating through the shadows, calling up creatures who had been hiding in the hollows, urging them to hoot and holler to populate the lonesome night.

That didgeridoo played a tune similar to one I had heard on the Hugh River, of red gums and ghost gums and galahs, of nightjars and dry winds. I came to understand that after tens of thousands of years of aborigines falling asleep to the sonic landscapes of desert eucalyptus forests, it was no miracle at all that the same aesthetic had found its way into their music.

BRING THE FAUNAL SYMPHONY HOME

I was back in my own desert following August, wandering around in the hills above a small village when the sun began to slip behind the mountains. It had rained hard recently, and the *charco* reservoir had filled to the brim, enticing egrets and king-fishers and plovers to stay in the heart of the desert longer than usual.

My wife and I walked down from a lava ridge above the *charco,* and just before sunset, a double rainbow arched over the entire scene. But that was not what riveted our attention. As darkness began to gain on us, something was moving around our feet. Was the ground itself vibrating, like grain shaking in an automatic sifter?

Then we heard them, tens of thousands of them—recently metamorphosed toads, bleating and bumping into one another. Dozens per square yard, they covered the banks of the reservoir, the lava ridge, and the trail back into the village. As darkness thickened, we also heard the rising chorus of their parents—Couch's spadefoot toads—sounding like an endless herd of sheep coming in for roundup.

Down below the ridge, dozens of headlights were streaming toward a ceremonial grounds. A line of ashes had been drawn around a huge arena, with a ramada or bower erected, facing east, at its western edge. A fire was built, a recently hunted javelina was hung in a gunnysack from a forked tree trunk, and a wild bunch of musicians and dancers assembled. Then five men came up and knelt in a line behind the fire, placed notched wooden sticks upon the ground, and began to rub raspers across them, singing at the same time. The rasping had a timbre identical to the croaking of the toads, and the deep, gruff voices of the singers added to the effect. I could not understand the words, but I heard the gratitude in those voices: gratitude that the rains had arrived, that the crops had come up, that the birds had returned, and that the *javelina* had fattened up in time to become the sacramental meal for the community assembled to sing their songs. The abundance of the summer had been assured once again, and everyone was grateful. Their songs lasted all night long, as lightning flashed around them. Now I knew that human, amphibian, or insect music accompanied each other not only in the deserts of Australia, but in my American desert home as well.

RE-STORYING A RAVAGED LAND

Every year, the first time I hear vermilion flycatchers in the leafed-out foliage of cottonwoods and willows, I know that spring has come again to the Sonoran Desert. I hear a *tut-tut, tiddly-zing,* then watch a gorgeous crimson bird sally out from a catkin-laden branch to catch its insect prey. It hovers a moment like a butterfly, swallows, then sashays back again to the safety of the canopy.

I suppose such sights and sounds cannot be found everywhere across the desert floor—they're pretty much limited to the ribbonlike riparian corridors of cottonwoods, willows, and sycamores that grow along stretches where water trickles to the surface of the meandering floodplains. If the winter has been cold enough to burn off other trees' leaves, or if it has been dry enough to leave the ocotillos barren and gray, spring restores life to them through the chorus of orioles, warblers, tanagers, hummingbirds, and flycatchers.

In eastern Sonora, the first flush of foliage on cottonwoods and willows has added significance. For a farmer in the villages of Cucurpe, Mazocahui, and Moctezuma, it means that the new cuttings for his hedgerows have taken root. He plants these cuttings on the exposed edges of his *milpa,* edges recently cut by El Niño downpours. The torrential floods of late autumn can churn up his corn fields and shift the courses of meandering rivers. If he has no erosion control set in place, such floods can leave a farmer a mess so awful that he will have to deal with it for years to come.

A few years before, however, this farmer had planted another hedge along the edge of his field, a few feet in from the gravelly riverbank. He had pruned the five-foot-long branches of cottonwoods nearby, trimmed their branchlets off with quick chops from his machete, and stuck them in the gravelly ground to root. Between these instant saplings, he wove a layer of smaller branches to make a brush fence. The next time a flood came, this *cerco tejido*—or woven fence—acted like a sieve, breaking the force of any floods that surged that high, letting the river-carried sediment filter out into his field.

"The trees and woven branches accept the floodwater and make it tame," the farmer told Thomas Sheridan and me once while we were visiting him in his fields. *Agua manza*—because his trees had tamed the flood, he ended up gaining rather than losing soil from his fields. And the trees of his living fence, all fertilized and irrigated, grew tall enough to lure vermilion flycatchers the next spring.

I have walked with elderly Sonorans out among the curving lines of cottonwoods edging their fields, where each hedge can prompt a story of a storm, a flood, an erosive event, a healing of scars, and a planting of more protective trees in their stead. One farmer I know can rattle off the years of great floods that have come within his own life span, as well as those that came during his father's time tending the land: 1887, 1890, 1905, 1914, 1915, 1926, 1940, 1961, 1977, and 1983. Farmers in other villages nearby sing much the same litany.

They can point to trees they helped plant after each inundation. They can read the growth on the floodplain as a living record of landmark floods and the patterns of recovery that followed. For them, those trees are what the notched calendar sticks are to the O'odham, where each groove serves as a mnemonic prompt to a memorable episode in community history: a bumper crop, a searing drought, or a roiling, rampaging tragedy.

Learning to read aloud the stories told by those rows of trees is what makes Sonoran farmboys literate. Learning how to plant and tend trees that bring warbling birds is another cultural skill. It tells each man that he can be a participant in the running of the desert river, can dance with its meanders, and sing with its birds. A gallery forest in the heart of the desert is no silent, static partner—it quakes and creaks to a larger music, a symphony so complex it has even incorporated some minor tunes intoned by humans.

Ecologist Daniel Botkin has written that this naturally improvised symphony "is by its very essence discordant, created from the simultaneous movements of many tones . . . flowing along many scales. . . . [It is] a symphony at some times harsh and at some times pleasing."

I, for one, cannot easily imagine how I could ever sit back and just listen to that symphony indefinitely; sooner or later, I must admit that even the unconscious tapping of my feet makes me a player, a part of the orchestra. And so, in adding my voice to those around me, I have chosen to be a choirboy in the desert chorus, and not to pretend that I am only an onlooker. I am part of the jam.

By making that choice, I have joined the ranks of a motley band of field scientists who dance to the tune called ecological restoration. That band both works and plays at reintroducing endangered plants and animals to habitats where they formerly occurred, and attempts to recover the vibrancy that those habitats once had. It is as much an art as a science, for it allows us to improvise, to listen to the land, to intuit where the harmonics of a natural community are going, as well as where they have been. We sing over the wounds left on this earth, and attempt to heal them. We recycle the oldest songs and stories in place, passing them on to the next generation.

We are learning of the need to restore not only the physical aspects of habitats, but the cultural commitment to protect, to heal, to let the wildness of living communities continue to evolve. Like the Seri hunter-gatherer or the Sonoran farmer, we must be encouraged to listen, live, and work like natives of our particular homeland, and to pass that work on to the next generation.

To restore any place, we must also begin to re-story it, to make it the lesson of our legends, festivals, and seasonal rites. Story is the way we encode deep-seeded values into our culture. Ritual is the way we enact them. We must ritually plant the cottonwood and willow poles in winter to be able to share the sounds of the vermilion flycatcher during the rites of spring. By replenishing the land with our stories, we let the many wild voices around us guide the restoration work we do. The stories will outlast us. When such voices are firmly rooted, the floods of modern technological change—of border-blasting radios and all-night pornography shows—won't ever have a chance to dislodge them from this earth.

Arrowhead and bullet found at campsite used by hunters for centuries

Crossing open ground, Camino del Diablo

Finding the water at Tule Tank, Camino del Diablo

Standing before signs of passage, Painted Rocks

First solstice, Phoenix

NOTES

Preface: Desert Follies and Borderline Fools

The epigrams quoted at the start of the preface are from Alfredo Vea, Jr., *La Maravilla* (Dutton, New York, 1993), and from his mythic counterpart in Sonora, Beto Nolosvea. My definitions of desert come from William Little, H. W. Fowler, and Jessie Colton, *The Shorter Oxford English Dictionary* (Oxford University Press, New York, 1973). I play devil's advocate with a quote from the delightful classic by Edward Abbey, *Desert Solitaire* (McGraw-Hill, New York, 1968). However, I could just as easily have drawn upon some vulnerable phrase in other desert classics, such as those written by Joseph Wood Krutch, *The Best Nature Writing of Joseph Wood Krutch* (William Morrow, New York, 1970), or Mary Austin, *The Land of Little Rain* (Houghton, Mifflin, Boston, 1903). For our own earlier contributions to discussions of desert landscapes, see Mark Klett and Denis Johnson, *Traces of Eden: Travels in the Desert Southwest* (Godine, Boston, 1986); Mark Klett, *Revealing Territory* (University of New Mexico Press, Albuquerque, 1992); Gary Paul Nabhan, *The Desert Smells Like Rain* (North Point Press, San Francisco, 1982); and Gary Paul Nabhan and Paul Mirocha, *Gathering the Desert* (University of Arizona Press, Tucson, 1985).

Rescuing What's on the Other Side

The epigrams quoted are from Walter Goldschmidt's foreword to Carlos Castaneda, *The Teachings of Don Juan: A Yaqui Way of Knowledge* (Simon and Schuster, New York, 1973), pp. 9–10, and from Pancho Norteado, a neighbor of sorts. The quote about crossing the border is from Graham Greene, *Another Mexico* (Viking, New York, 1982). If you don't believe in mirages caused by the Novaya Zemyla effect, see Aden and Marjorie Meinel, *Sunsets, Twilights, and Evening Skies* (Cambridge University Press, Cambridge, 1983). The quote on the borderlands as a separate country is from Douglas Kent Hall, *The Border: Life on the Line* (Abbeville Press, New York, 1988). That theme is also explored in a novel by Carlos Fuentes, *Cristóbal Nonato* (Fondo de Cultura Economica, México City, México, 1987). My favorite border book remains the one by Alan Weisman and Jay Dusard, *La Frontera* (Harcourt Brace Jovanovich, New York, 1986). The discussions with O'odham farmers occurred while I was working on my dissertation, "Papago Fields: Arid Land Ethnobotany and Agroecology" (University of Arizona, Tucson, 1983), and assisting them with their fields.

Cryptic Cacti on the Borderline

The epigrams quoted are from the great precursor of magical realism, Jose Lezama Lima, *Las Eras Imaginarias* (Editoriál Fundamentos, Madrid, 1971), and from the mythic Ironwood John of Papaguería, Juan Hoidkam, whose works have not yet been published. The ironwood ecology story has been told in considerable technical detail in a monograph of four studies that I coedited for the Ironwood Alliance: Gary Paul Nabhan and John Carr, eds., *Ironwood: An Ecological and Cultural Keystone of the Sonoran Desert,* Conservation International Occasional Papers in Conservation Biology No. 1 (Washington, D.C., 1994). This monograph features the work of Mexican ecologists Alberto Búrquez and Humberto Suzan, among others. See also Peter Steinhart and Tupper Ansel Blake, *Dos Aguilas/ Two Eagles* (University of California Press, Berkeley, 1994), and Gary Paul Nabhan, "Desert Rescuers," *World Monitor* 7, number 5, pp. 36–41. For related technical studies, the best overview of the Kunkaak use of ironwood is Richard S. Felger and Mary Beck Moser, *People of the Desert and Sea: Ethnobotany of the Seri Indians* (University of Arizona, Tucson, 1985), and a review of the nurse plant ecology of borderland plants is Gary Paul Nabhan, "Nurse Plant Ecology of Threatened Desert Plants," in *Conservation and Management of Rare and Endangered Plants,* ed. T. Elias (California Native Plant Society, Sacramento, 1987), pp. 203–9.

Hanging Out the Dirty Laundry

The epigrams are quoted from Gerald Vizenor, *Landfill Meditation: Crossblood Stories* (University Presses of New England, Wesleyan, 1991), and from El Pepenador, who privately prints messages on recycled paper behind a bush outside the Sonoyta city limits. The reigning book of garbage—notwithstanding A. R. Ammons's long poem—remains the anthropological study by William Rathje and Cullen Murphy, *Rubbish: The Archaeology of Garbage* (Harper Perrenial, New York, 1992). A moving piece on life in the *dompes* of Baja California has been written by Luis Alberto Urrea, *Across the Wire: Life and Hard Times on the Mexican Border* (Anchor/Doubleday, New York, 1993). The story of beef jerky left in the hide is from Raphael Pumpelly, *Across America and Asia* (Leypoldt and Holt, New York, 1870), and from his field notes published in 1918: *My Reminiscences* (Henry Holt, New York). Edward Abbey complained about Sonora in "Down There in Sonora," in *Down the River* (E. P. Dutton, New York, 1982), pp. 149–53. For the dump heap theory, see Carl O. Sauer, *Seeds, Spades, Hearths, and Herds* (MIT Press, Cambridge, 1969).

Searching for the Cure

The epigrams quoted come from Laura Esquivel, *Como Agua Para Chocolate* (Doubleday, New York, 1989), and from Ana Castillo, *So Far from God* (Norton, New York, 1993). For an overview of Mexican-American healing traditions, see Margarita Artschwager Kay, "Health and Illness in a Mexican American Barrio," in *Ethnic Medicine in the Southwest,* ed. Edward H. Spicer (University of Arizona Press, Tucson, 1977), pp. 101–67. La Viuda wishes that her name and village not be divulged; otherwise, these events are as they happened.

Shuttling Across: Weaving a Desert Serape

The epigrams are quoted from Carlos Fuentes, *Gringo Viejo* (Fondo de Cultura Económica, Mexico City, 1985), and from William Langeswieche, *Cutting for Sign* (Pantheon, New York, 1993). I was helped in setting on the pilgrimage and in interpreting Sonoran folk Catholicism by James S. Griffith, *Beliefs and Holy Places: A Spiritual Geography of the Pimería Alta* (University of Arizona Press, Tucson, 1992). Another of my own pilgrimages in the Sonoran Desert was recorded in Gary Paul Nabhan, "The Movable O'odham Feast of San Francisco," *Native Peoples* 4, no. 2 (1991): 28–34. Discussions of environmental change come from various sources, including: Amadeo Rea, *Once a River: Bird Life and Habitat Changes on the Middle Gila* (University of Arizona Press, Tucson, 1980); Karen Reichhardt, *Natural Vegetation of Casa Grande Ruins National Monument, Arizona* (National Park Service Cooperative Park Study Unit of the University of Arizona Technical Report NPS/WRUA/NRTR 92–45, Tucson, 1992); Robert Webb and Julio Betancourt, *Climatic Variability and Flood Frequency of the Santa Cruz River, Pima County, Arizona,* U.S. Geological Survey Water Supply Paper 2379 (Washington, D.C., 1992); Julio L. Betancourt and Ray M. Turner, "Historic Arroyo-Cutting and Subsequent Channel Changes at the Congress Street Crossing, Santa Cruz River," in *Arid Lands: Today and Tomorrow,* ed. E. E. Whitehead (Westview Press, Boulder, Colo., 1988), pp. 1353–71. Details of southern Arizona history are taken from the following: Nicholas J. Bleser, *Tumacácori from Rancheria to National Monument* (Southwest Parks and Monuments Association, Tucson, 1989); Neil B. Carmony and David E. Brown, *Man and Wildlife in Arizona* (Arizona Game and Fish, Phoenix, 1982); and Susan Spater et al., eds., *Voices from the Pimería Alta* (Pimería Alta Historical Society, Nogales, 1991).

When the Desert Dances the Sonoran Shuffle

The epigrams are quotes from Frank Russell (and Jose Luis Brennan), *The Pima Indians* (University of Arizona, Tucson, 1975), and from Joaquin Murrieta, who still stomp-dances to Sonoran *corridos* from Chiapas to California.

Finding the Hidden Garden

The epigrams are quotes from Jimmie Dale Gilmore and David Hammond, "Where Are You Going?" on the Gilmore recording *Spinning Around the Sun* (Elektra/Warner Brothers, New York, 1993)—the lyrics are copyrighted by Jade EG Music and Hydra's Teeth Music, BMI— and from Octavio Paz, "Piedra del Sol/Sunstone," in *The Collected Poems of Octavio Paz,* ed.

Eliot Weinburger (New Directions, New York, 1987), p. 3. I have also drawn from Howard Scott Gentry, "The Man/Agave Symbiosis," *Saguaroland Bulletin* 29, no. 7 (1975): 80–84; Howard Scott Gentry, *The Agave Family in Sonora,* USDA Agricultural Handbook No. 399 (Beltsville, Md., 1972); and Howard Scott Gentry, *Agaves of Continental North America* (University of Arizona Press, Tucson, 1982). Much of the *Agave murpheyi* work with Wendy Hodgson and others remains in press, but we have published one article: Wendy Hodgson, Gary Paul Nabhan, and Liz Ecker, "Conserving Rediscovered Agave Cultivars," *Agave* 3 (1989): 9–11. See also Suzanne K. Fish, Paul R. Fish, Charles Miksicek, and John Madsen, "Prehistoric Agave Cultivation in Southern Arizona," *Desert Plants* 7, no. 2 (1985): 107–12. A volume being edited by Suzanne Fish and James Parsons on agave uses in the Americas is forthcoming from the University of Arizona Press and includes definitive data from Wendy Hodgson, Rick DeLamater, James Hickey, and me. With regard to "hidden gardens" in American wilderness areas, see Kat Anderson and Gary Paul Nabhan, "Gardeners in Eden," *Wilderness* 55, no. 184 (1991): 27–31.

Re-storying the Sonorous Land

The epigrams are quoted from Juan Mata's basket song translated in Edward Moser's essay, "Seri Basketry," *The Kiva* 38, nos. 3–4 (1973): 105–140; and from Pat Mora, "The Border: A Glare of Truth," in *Nepantla* (University of New Mexico Press, Albuquerque, 1993). See also Pat Mora, *Borders* (Arté Publico Press, Houston, 1983). This essay was inspired by the work of Steven Feld, John Henry Adams, and Jack Loeffler recording "sonic landscapes" of different bioregions. For example, see Steven Feld, *Sound and Sentiment: Birds, Weeping, Poetics, and Song in Kaluli Expression* (University of Pennsylvania Press, Philadelphia, 1982), and Steven Feld, recorder, *Voices of the Rainforest* (Rykodisc, Salem, Mass., 1991). Regarding Sonoran floodplain management and restoration, see: Gary Paul Nabhan and Thomas Sheridan, "Living Fencerows of the Río San Miguel, Sonora: Traditional Technology for Floodplain Management," *Human Ecology* 5, no. 2 (1977): 97–111; Thomas Sheridan and Gary Paul Nabhan, "Traditional Technology for Floodplain Management in Sonora, Mexico," pp. 74–82 in K. James DeCook and Kenneth E. Foster, eds., *Proceedings of the Symposium on Flood Monitoring and Management* (Arizona Water Resources Association, Tucson, 1979); and Thomas Sheridan's excellent book, *Where the Dove Calls* (University of Arizona Press, Tucson, 1988). I have also quoted Daniel Botkin, *Discordant Harmonies* (Oxford University Press, Oxford, 1990). In addition, I am indebted to two essays that I first encountered in the special issue of *Antaeus* devoted to nature writing: Leslie Marmon Silko, "Landscape, History, and the Pueblo Imagination," and Keith H. Basso, pp. " 'Stalking the Stories': Names, Places, and Moral Narratives among the Western Apaches," in *On Nature,* ed. Daniel Halpern (North Point Press, Berkeley, 1986), pp. 83–94 and 95–116, respectively.

ACKNOWLEDGMENTS

We're grateful for the opportunity to work in tandem, as writer and photographic artist, on the same themes and metaphors, reinforcing each other's work in ways we could hardly imagine at the onset of this project. For helping us realize this opportunity, we thank our agents, Tim Schaffner and Victoria Shoemaker, and our families.

I would like to recognize the editors and publishers who demonstrated interest in earlier drafts of these essays. Aina Niemela edited "Cryptic Cacti on the Borderline" for *Orion,* and Tom Lyon helped improve an updated version for the Texas A&M anthology *On Nature's Terms.* Mike Katakis and Tom Christensen published a version of "Hanging Out the Dirty Laundry" in *Sacred Trusts* at Mercury House, and Doug Biggers printed the same in the *Tucson Weekly.* Jack Shoemaker of North Point Press originally commissioned "Shuttling Across" for a book-length project and forgave me when it found another form. "Re-storying the Sonorous Land" originally appeared in butchered form in *Sierra* and was later restored by Bill Jordan for *Restoration and Management Notes* and by Kevin Dahl for *The Seedhead News.* "The Sonoran Shuffle" was called "When the Desert Dances" in the 1993 *Sierra Club Wildlife Calendar.* David Yetman originally inspired me to write "Finding the Hidden Garden" for a special 1994 issue of the *Journal of the Southwest* on the legacy of Howard Scott Gentry.

Because I seldom travel alone or think in a vacuum, I wish to acknowledge the many friends, elders, scholars, activists, farmers, and desert rats whose companionship helped shape these essays. In particular, I thank the following "elders" of various Sonoran Desert cultures: Delores Lewis, Frances Manual, "la Viuda" the *curandera,* Casimiro Sanchez, Adalberto Cruz, the late Howard Scott Gentry, Marie Gentry, Julian Hayden, Chapo Barnet, Juan Arguelles, Louise Havier, Angelita Enriquez, Anita Antone, Laura Kerman, and Chico Suni. The following friends were companions and teachers on forays into the desert: Thomas Sheridan, Jim Hills, Humberto Suzan, Caroline Wilson, Adrian Hendricks, Culver Cassa, Big Jim Griffith, Richard Felger, Nancy Ferguson, Tom Orum, Wendy Hodgson, the late Rick DeLamater, Susan Spater, Nick Bleser, Suzanne Fish, Charlie Miksicek, Julio Betancourt, Ginger Harmon, Mrill Ingram, Barney T. Burns, John Harris, Daniel Preston, Brenda Sekaquaptewa, Chris Keith, Sara St. Antoine, Lisa Famolare, Mark Plotkin, Roger Swain, Kat Anderson, Jack Loeffler, Conrad Bahre, Dustin and Laura Nabhan, José Enriquez, Fillman Bell, Alberto Burquez, and Floyd Flores. I thank Alberto Rios for guiding my readings in magical realism, while Joe Wilder, Richard Nelson, Jesus Garcia, Amadeo Rea, Wendy Laird, and Dick Kamp offered me other desert borderland readings. My ability to keep in the borderland groove was greatly enhanced by hearing the multilingual music of Flaco Jimenez, Ryland Cooder, Butch Hancock, Southern Scratch, the Joaquin Brothers, Los Lobos, Tish Hinojosa, John Thompson and the Organ Donors, Hector and the Javelinas, Rosie Flores, Travis Edmonson, and Linda Ronstadt. Andy Robinson, Victoria Shoemaker, Caroline Wilson, David Lee, Terry Tempest Williams, and Sara St. Antoine provided editorial guidance and inspiration when I was floundering like a brine shrimp in a soon-to-evaporate *tinaja*. *Mil gracias, amigos.*

I have been lucky enough to have had the support of a MacArthur Fellowship, a Pew Scholarship in Conservation and Environment, as well as Visiting Writer positions at Arizona State University, University of California at Santa Cruz, and the Arizona-Sonora Desert Museum. Native Seeds SEARCH, Conservation International, Jim Hills, Julia Roberts, Roy Long, John Hay, the Overbrook Foundation, ARCO Foundation, Robidaux Foundation, and Miguel Aleman Foundation have all assisted the desert conservation efforts of our "Ironwood Alliance." Thanks to all involved.

—Gary Nabhan

I thank my partners in travel: Richard Laugharn, Don Leddick, Ian VanColler, Linda Connor, David Hurn, and Dean Eppler. Most photographers depend on the kindness of strangers, and I am particularly grateful to those in Querobabi, Guadalupe, and Sonoyta, Sonora, and to the last man living in the bombing range, Chico Suni. I also wish to acknowledge the support of the School of Art at Arizona State University for allowing me a leave of absence while pursuing this project.

Finally, the love and support of three women who counted the most: that of my wife, Emily Matyas, and my daughters, Lena and Natalie.

—Mark Klett